Linda McCartney
on Tour

Linda McCartney
on Tour

OVER 200 MEAT-FREE DISHES FROM AROUND THE WORLD

LINDA MCCARTNEY

PHOTOGRAPHER
DEBBIE PATTERSON

FOOD CONSULTANT
ROSAMOND RICHARDSON

HOME ECONOMIST
JANE SUTHERING

A LITTLE, BROWN BOOK
LITTLE, BROWN AND COMPANY
BOSTON • NEW YORK • LONDON

I dedicate this book to my delicious family
who are everything to me

First edition

ISBN 0-316-63979-6

A CIP catalogue for this book is available from the British Library

Food stylist: Jane Suthering
Prop stylist: Tessa Evelegh
Designer: Janet James
Editorial team: Julia Charles, Mary McCartney, Louise Morris, Sue Prochnik, Elaine Steer

Published simultaneously in the United States of America by Bulfinch Press, an imprint and trademark of Little, Brown and Company (Inc.), in Great Britain by Little, Brown and Company (UK)

The author would like to thank Paul, Heather, Mary, Stella, James, Louise, Sue, Elaine, Helge, Sharon, Pat, Alistair, Robby and team, Bo, Roger, Joanne, Dav, Kim, Fred, Nick, Monique, Laura and Donald, Shelagh, Marie, Tim and team, Julia and team, Carol Judy and team, John and Louise, Zoë and Elizabeth and everyone who helped and shared a veggie recipe

The publishers would like to thank Conran Octopus for permission to reproduce the Debbie Patterson photograph used on page 1 which originally appeared in *Slim and Healthy Mediterranean.*

Printed and bound in Italy

CONTENTS

V INDICATES A VEGAN DISH

 Vegetarianism is now the biggest food trend of the century and I, for one, couldn't be more thrilled! Since I wrote my previous cookbooks more and more people have taken responsibility for their health and their planet by adopting a meat-free diet – at the present growth rate it is predicted that we will ALL be veggie by the year 2050, so if you don't want to be left behind now is the time to get started!

If you are still considering your choices and need a little more encouragement, take time to think about the following facts for a minute or two. Recent statistics have revealed that a life-long non-meat-eater saves around 760 chickens, 5 cows, 20 pigs, 29 sheep, 46 turkeys, 7 rabbits and over half a tonne of fish. Just imagine standing in a farm and looking at all these lives that you, as a meat-eater, will indirectly have ended in your own lifetime! I can't think of a more literal and convincing argument, and nothing outweighs the rewards of living a guilt-free and compassionate life.

Another important factor, which has no doubt contributed to the boom in the number of new veggies, is meat poisoning. This has been one of the biggest political and social issues of recent years – with the alarming increase in cases of BSE and CJD, eating meat has become a risky business. There is really no need to take any risks with your health in our modern and civilised society and you reserve the right to eat food which is clean and pure. Curiously, many people still believe that their health will suffer if they cut meat out of their diet; most doctors and nutritionists would not agree.

Today, more than ever before, becoming a veggie is one of the easiest and most positive decisions you can make. You will be spoilt for choice in shops and restaurants and, thanks to the wonders of modern food technology, even the traditional meat-eater who loves burgers, sausages and bacon rashers no longer has to make any sacrifices.

As you can see, there are many good reasons to go veggie but I've been saving one of the best until last and that is that meat-free food is delicious! It is exciting and modern. What I'm aiming to show you in this book is that cutting out meat doesn't mean leaving just the veg – it's about learning a different way of cooking and adopting a whole new approach to the way that you choose to feed yourself. The first thing you'll discover as you start following my recipes is your tastebuds – there's a whole world of flavours out there! I've included many of my favourite dishes from around the world – memorable meals that I've enjoyed with family and friends over the years – on holiday as well as at work. The more I've researched this book, the more I have come to realise how much we can learn by looking at other cultures where meat and dairy products have never been plentiful (or for religious reasons not widely eaten) and how, with a little creative use of herbs, spices and exotic ingredients, meat-free feasts can be created from the simplest of foods.

Even if you find cooking a little daunting, my new collection of recipes is guaranteed to bring out the cook in you. Don't be afraid to adapt my recipes to suit your own tastes and remember that veggie cooking is all about having fun, being creative and doing something not just for yourself but for your planet and the animals you share it with.

Linda McCartney
April 1998

NUTRITION FOR VEGETARIANS

What is a vegetarian?

Even though all the surveys tell us that the number of vegetarians and non-meat-eaters is growing by leaps and bounds, many people still do not really know what being a vegetarian means. This is partly because there are a number of different kinds – demi-veggies, lacto/ovo veggies, and vegans are the main three. A true veggie will not eat any food which is, or contains, the flesh of any animal, bird or fish. Nor will they eat anything which has been made from any body part of an animal, bird or fish. This could be lard or suet (made from animal fat), gelatine (made from animal bones, hooves and hide or fish bones), rennet in cheese (it can be made from calves' stomachs), finings used to clear wine (can be made from egg or gelatine), some additives which can be derived from animal fats, or vitamin or mineral supplements in gelatine casings. However, vegetarians will eat animal produce – eggs or dairy products which may come from animals but are not actually part of their bodies. These vegetarians are also known as 'lacto (milk)/ovo (egg) vegetarians'.

Vegans, on the other hand, will not eat anything which has come from an animal at all. Many maintain that if you do not eat animals themselves, then it is not logical to eat anything which comes from an animal such as milk and dairy products, eggs and honey.

Vegetarian nutrition

Even though so many people are now reducing the amount of meat they eat or switching to a vegetarian or demi-veg diet, some people (parents especially) are still worried that a vegetarian or vegan diet cannot provide all the nourishment that a body needs to remain healthy. This couldn't be further from the truth. A well-balanced meat-free diet is now widely regarded to be the healthiest choice. So let us look at the nutrients in turn. (For a more detailed guide to nutrient sources, see the chart on pages 12 and 13.)

Protein

Most people in the Western world eat nearly twice as much protein as they actually need. Pulses, nuts and seeds are all good sources of protein, although the best, from a vegetarian point of view, is soya, as it is the only non-animal food which contains all the amino acids. In 'nutrition speak' it is a 'complete protein'.

Carbohydrates

Starchy carbohydrate foods (known as complex carbohydrates) are the basis of a balanced diet and vegetarian food has loads of them. Cereals, grains, pulses and root vegetables are widely used in many vegetarian dishes, so there are no worries there.

Fats

Most people are concerned about eating too much fat, not too little. Vegetarians are one step ahead here, as they have cut out a number of 'saturated' animal fats. However, cheese and milk-eating vegetarians need to keep an eye on their general dairy intake. It is a great temptation to fill up on cheese, yoghurts and other milk based foods, some of which have a very high fat content.

Fibre

Unlike fat, most people tend to eat too little rather than too much fibre, but here again vegetarians are ahead, as those eating lots of starchy carbohydrates (see left) will automatically be getting a good daily intake of fibre.

Vitamins and minerals

Most vegetarian foods are a good source of vitamins and minerals.

Calcium is the mineral which is of most concern to vegans who do not eat dairy products. However, tofu (soya bean curd) is a rich source of calcium, as are green leafy vegetables. Many soya milks are also fortified with extra calcium. Iron is also to be found in tofu, pulses, green leafy vegetables and dried fruits such as prunes and apricots.

Wheat germ, wholegrain cereals, pulses, soya, nuts, seeds and seaweed, all widely used in vegetarian cooking, are all good sources of chromium, copper, iodine, magnesium, manganese, molybdenum, phosphorus, potassium, selenium and zinc, so vegetarians need have no concerns about going short on minerals!

Shopping for vegetarian foods

Vegetarian shopping is no different from any other shopping if you are just buying raw materials such as fruits, vegetables or pulses. It becomes just a little bit harder when you buy ready-made products – from mayonnaise to ready-meals. Many composite dishes use animal products in their ingredients, but if you do not read the label carefully – and knowledgeably – you may not realise this.

Reading labels

Beware of hidden ingredients. Once you have got used to reading labels and memorised some of the most important ingredients, recognising animal ingredients will become second nature when you shop.

ANIMAL FATS

These are used in lots of products, both food and household. Biscuits and bought cakes often contain animal fats, so unless the label specifies 'vegetable fats' do not buy them. Check the labels on pastry products too – the pastry is usually made with vegetable fat, but not always.

SPREADS

Check the ingredients lists carefully before you buy your spread. Many include dairy products (whey or casein) which will not be a problem if you are just vegetarian, but will be if you are vegan.

Make sure that you buy non-hydrogenated spreads. Although hydrogenation does not involve animal products, it is a process by which vegetable oils are heated to a very high temperature so that they harden and can be used as spreads. Unfortunately the changes in the oil caused by this process makes it much more difficult for the body to absorb the fat and may even harm our bodies.

RENNET

Rennet is what separates the curds from the whey in cheese-making and it used to be made from the lining of calves' stomachs. In fact, the majority of cheesemakers today uses a vegetable-based rennet but you cannot be sure unless it specifies 'vegetable rennet' on the packet.

GELATINE OR GELLING AGENTS

Most gelatine is made from animals hides, hooves and bones and from fish bones. Gelatine crops up in all kinds of products, savoury and, especially, sweet, so check all ready-made desserts and yoghurts.

If you take vitamin supplements, you should also check whether the capsules have been made from gelatine – there are vegetarian equivalents. And check the source of the vitamin itself as several have animal derivations.

ADDITIVES

Take care over emulsifiers E470 to E479. They are made from fatty acids which can be of animal or vegetable origin but they rarely tell you which.

DAIRY PRODUCTS AND EGGS

These will not be a problem if you are vegetarian but if you are vegan and need to avoid them you have some more learning to do. Dairy and egg products are very widely used in food manufacture so watch out for any of the following:

DAIRY:	EGGS:
Casein/caseinates	Albumin/conalbumin or
Ghee	ovalbumin
Lactose	Ovomucoid/ovoglobulin
Whey	Vitellin/vitellenin

SAUCES AND STOCKS

You need to check the labels carefully on ready made sauces and stocks. Some, like Bovril, have very obvious animal ingredients. Others like mayonnaise (eggs) or Worcestershire sauce (anchovies) may not be so clear.

READY-MEALS

As the number of vegetarians grows so does the range of meat-free foods on offer to us – especially ready-meals. Many major manufacturers now produce vegetarian versions of all the standard dishes such as lasagne or chilli. Others make vegetarian burgers and bangers and of course my own range of meat-free meals is expanding all the time. Many Indian, Chinese or Far Eastern dishes will also be vegetarian but unless it is produced as a vegetarian range, you should still check the label carefully.

Alternatives to dairy products

For many years, if you did not want to eat dairy products, all you were offered was rather 'chalky' tasting soya milk. However, things are a lot better today.

Soya milks and yoghurts now come in a wide range of flavours, they are fortified with vitamins and minerals, and organic brands are available. Soya cream, which tastes not unlike real cream and is excellent in cooked dishes as well as on desserts, is now easily available. Tofu (soya bean curd) can be found soft (silken) or set like a cheese and you can buy it plain, smoked or marinated. It is excellent in a wide range of casseroles, stir-fries, salads and sandwiches.

Textured Vegetable Protein or TVP uses soya to create a meat-type product which is often almost indistinguishable from the real thing and is excellent for those many vegetarians who actually like the texture and taste of meat but do not like the idea of eating it.

Meanwhile, medical research suggests that soya is an excellent food to eat to protect you against a whole range of other twentieth-century diseases.

And for those who do not actually like the taste of soya milk as a drink or on their breakfast cereal, you can now also buy rice milk (sweet but pleasant) and oatmilk. For cooking, coconut milk (which can be bought tinned or made by boiling desiccated coconut in water) is also excellent.

Organic produce

Eating organic food is one of the most important contributions any of us can make to save the planet. Over 25,000 tons of pesticides, herbicides and fungicides are used in Britain alone every year.

In one sense, all food is 'organic' because it has come from plants or animals. However, for the past fifty years or so 'organic' has been used specifically to describe food grown without artificial fertilizers or pesticides and in a way that produces optimum quantities of food of high nutritional quality with minimal damage to the environment and wildlife. The term 'organic' is now protected by EC law and it means that the product has been rigorously inspected from the farm to the shop by an independent control body such as the Soil Association in the UK.

Organic farmers and producers employ cultivation and crop rotation systems in order to develop natural soil fertility. This means that the soil is enriched by composted manures, nitrogen fixing plants and naturally occurring minerals rather than by artificial fertilisers. In addition trees, hedgerows and field boundaries are planted and managed to prevent soil erosion and to encourage wildlife, which in turn encourages natural pest control and alleviates the need for toxic pesticides. Dairy products or eggs marked organic will have been provided by animals fed on organic grass, fodder or grain and they will not have been intensively farmed or injected with growth hormones or antibiotics.

Because it is not intensively farmed and because organic farmers are more interested in the health of their crops than getting every apple exactly the same shape as every other apple, organic fruits and vegetables may not look as perfect as non-organic – but they often taste a lot better!

Because organic farming is more labour intensive, there are still a relatively small number of organic farmers, and because the industry does not get much in the way of subsidies, organic produce can still be appreciably a little more expensive than ordinary produce, although prices are now starting to come down. Potatoes, carrots and onions are now fairly cheap and are a good way to test how much better organic food tastes.

If you want to buy organically – look for the Soil Assocation symbol on the packet, label or tag. Alternatively contact the Soil Association – Bristol House, 90 Victoria Street, Bristol BS1 6DF Tel. 0117 929 0661. They have a list of local organic growers many of whom run 'box' schemes, delivering a box of organic products to your door on a weekly basis. If your local health shop or supermarket doesn't stock organic produce, ask them for it. Supply creates demand and there is no better way to support the organic movement.

Eating out

There are very few restaurants now which do not offer some kind of vegetarian alternative. And you do not need to feel awkward about asking for it, as many people who are not veggies choose the vegetarian alternative as they find it lighter and healthier. However, it is still worth checking whether sauces, pastries and desserts have been made with vegetarian ingredients (no meat stocks, no animal fats, no gelatine).

But once again, if you are a vegan you need to be more careful as you cannot eat anything which has been cooked with butter, cream, cheese, yoghurt, eggs or honey.

If you are going to a meat-eating friend's home to eat, give them ample warning and let them rise to the challenge – you can always offer a few suggestions of your own.

Eating in

Meat eaters often claim that cooking vegetarian food is much harder than cooking meat-based food but I cannot think why. It is no more difficult to cook a veggie loaf and some side dishes than it is to cook roast beef and two veg! If you are having meat-eating friends in to eat with you don't think twice before serving them vegetarian food. There are so many delicious and exciting recipes for non-meat dishes in this book alone that the chances are that they will not even notice that they haven't eaten any meat!

The vegetarian larder

As any good cook knows, a well stocked larder is a great way to start.

Beans and pulses

Split peas, whole lentils and split lentils do not need to be soaked overnight, but it is recommended that you soak the other pulses for approximately 8–12 hours. The times given below are a rough guide, as cooking times can vary considerably depending on the age and origin of the crop. The first ten minutes' cooking of all except lentils and split peas should be done at a fast boil, uncovered, to destroy any toxic elements on the outer skin, except soya beans, which should boil hard for the first hour. Although lentils and split peas need not be soaked overnight, they will cook faster if they are first steeped in boiling water for 15–30 minutes. Drain before cooking them.

Once cooked, beans, peas and lentils keep well for several days in a covered container in the refrigerator, or they can be frozen and will still retain their flavour. Cool and open freeze them, then pack them in rigid containers and label them. For soups, a handful or two can be removed and put straight into the soup near the end of the cooking time. For salads, allow them to thaw for about an hour at room temperature or overnight in the fridge.

Aduki beans	45 minutes
Black-eyed beans	45–50 minutes
Black beans	50–60 minutes
Broad beans	1½ hours
Butter or lima beans	60–90 minutes
Cannellini beans	45–50 minutes
Flageolets	45–50 minutes
Haricot beans	50–60 minutes
Mung beans	30–45 minutes
Pinto beans	60–90 minutes
Red kidney beans	45–50 minutes
Soya beans	2–2½ hours
Chick peas	60–90 minutes
Whole green peas	60–90 minutes
Split peas	40–45 minutes
Whole lentils	30–45 minutes
Split lentils	15–30 minutes

Soya products

Soya beans are immensely useful to the vegetarian. Not only do they provide soya milk (made by boiling soya beans in water then straining it) and soya cream (made from soya milk), but tofu (soya bean curd), tempeh, miso, soya sauce and tamari (all seasonings or sauce made from fermented soya beans), soya margarine and oil (both healthy fats for cooking and spreading), soya flour (widely used in baking) and TVP or textured vegetable protein, which is used to provide the majority of 'meat' substitutes. TVP comes both chilled and frozen and can be used straight from the chiller or freezer. Other meat substitutes are made from wheat gluten or a myco-protein, which is mushroom in origin, and are very successful. Use them as you would TVP.

Soya milk and cream both come in Long Life versions, and there are dozens of different flavours of soya milk suitable for both drinking and cooking.

Tofu comes in soft (silken) or set textures and in a variety of flavours and can be added to casseroles, salads and many ethnic dishes.

Nuts and seeds

Always keep a good stock of nuts (almonds, brazil nuts, cashews, hazelnuts, pecans, peanuts, pine nuts, pistachios, walnuts). They can be added to almost any vegetarian dish either whole or crushed, as they are or toasted. Not only do they add lots of flavour and texture to the dish, but also plenty of vitamins and minerals. However, take care as they are also very calorific!

Seeds (pumpkin, sunflower, poppy, sesame) are equally useful for adding flavour and texture but, being lower in fat, are not as calorific, although just as nutritious, as nuts.

Fruit and vegetables

The other mainstay of the vegetarian diet should be fresh fruits and vegetables, ideally organic (see page 10). Root vegetables are wonderfully filling and keep very well. Most vegetables are excellent either cooked or raw and are extremely nutritious. Fresh fruits can be used fresh or cooked, on their own or in desserts.

Although fresh organic fruit and vegetables are ideal, it is well worth keeping some tinned and dried stocks in the cupboard for emergencies.

Tinned tomatoes are invaluable in any casserole, stew or sauce, while tinned sweetcorn, pimentos, artichoke hearts and olives make excellent and flavoursome additions to any vegetarian dish.

Dried fruits (raisins, sultanas, currants, prunes, apricots, figs) are great as snacks or mixed in with fresh fruits in a dessert or in cakes and baked goods.

Protein

Proteins are made up of amino acids and different foods contain different amino acids. The foods listed below are all good sources of protein although soya is the best as it contains all the amino acids that we need.

GOOD SOURCES

* *Soya products* – soya milk, tofu and TVP
* *Beans, peas and lentils*
* *Cereals & whole grains* – rice, oatmeal, whole-wheat flour
* *Nuts & seeds* – including dishes made from nuts and seeds ie. tahini, hummus
* *Dairy products* – milk, butter, cheese
* *Eggs*

Fat

A certain amount of fat is absolutely essential to allow your body to function properly but it must be the right kind of fat. Fats fall into three main categories.
Saturated fats. These can be bad for us if we eat too much of them as they convert into cholesterol in our bodies, which can lead to heart disease. Saturated fats come mainly from animal foods. Full-fat milk, butter, hard cheese and some nuts.

Polyunsaturated and **monounsaturated fats** provide essential fatty acids that the body needs. (Polyunsaturated fats come from liquid oils and are sometimes 'hydrogenated'. However, the hydrogenation changes the nature of the fat so that the body cannot use it in the same way as a normal polyunsaturated fat.)

GOOD SOURCES

* *Cold pressed vegetable oils* – olive, sunflower, soya, corn
* *Non-hydrogenated spreads & margarines*
* *Nuts*
* *Avocados*

Carbohydrates

Starchy carbohydrate foods (known as complex carbohydrates) are the basis of a balanced diet.

Sugary carbohydrate foods (known as simple carbohydrates) have little nutritional value and lots of calories, so are to be avoided. You will find them in sugar, sweets, chocolate, cakes and biscuits made with refined flours and sugars.

GOOD SOURCES

* *Beans, peas & lentils*
* *Whole grains, rices & cereals*
* *Pasta*
* *Most fresh fruit & vegetables, especially potatoes, root vegetables & bananas*

Fibre

Fibre is to be found in complex carbohydrates and is important for helping waste to pass rapidly through the digestive system.

GOOD SOURCES

* *Beans, peas & lentils*
* *Oats*
* *Dried fruits*
* *Wholegrains & wholemeal cereals*
* *Virtually all fresh fruits & vegetables, especially berry fruits, carrots & cabbage*

Vitamins

Our bodies need a small amount of each vitamin to function properly but apart from Vitamin D (which the body can manufacture itself from sunlight) they cannot make their own vitamins, so we need to get them from the food we eat.

VITAMIN A

Needed for healthy skin and good vision

GOOD SOURCES

* *Carrots*
* *Broccoli*
* *Green leafy vegetables*
* *Red & yellow peppers*
* *Dried apricots*
* *Melons & mangoes*
* *Dairy products*

B VITAMINS

8 different B vitamins help to release energy and essential nutrients.

GOOD SOURCES

* *Wholegrain cereals*
* *Yeast extract*
* *Nuts & seeds*
* *Wide range of fruits & vegetables, especially green vegetables, mushrooms, bananas & avocados*

VITAMIN B12

Needed for the formation of red blood cells and genetic material and protection of the nerves.

GOOD SOURCES

* *Yeast extract*
* *Seaweeds & alfalfa sprouts*
* *Fortified soya milk, margarine & breakfast cereals*
* *Fermented soya foods* – soya sauce, miso, tamari

VITAMIN C

Essential for the formation and maintenance of bones, teeth and tissue and overall health.
Since we cannot store Vitamin C in our bodies we need to eat Vitamin C-bearing foods on a daily basis. Vitamin C is destroyed by light and heat so it is better to eat at least some of your fruits and vegetables raw.

GOOD SOURCES

* *Citrus & berry fruits*
* *Kiwi fruit*
* *Red peppers*
* *Potatoes*
* *Tomatoes*

VITAMIN D

Needed for the absorption of calcium into the body. Vitamin D is manufactured by the body when exposed to sunlight, but it can also be found in some foods.

GOOD SOURCES

* *Eggs*
* *Fortified cereals*
* *Fortified margarine*

VITAMIN E

Needed for red blood cell formation, general healing and to protect the body against the harmful effects of free-radicals.

GOOD SOURCES

* *Nuts & seeds*
* *Vegetables oils & spreads*
* *Wheatgerm & whole grain cereals*
* *Avocados*

VITAMIN K

Vitamin K is needed for blood clotting and bone health, but at least half of our daily needs are manufactured by the body itself.

GOOD SOURCES

* *Green leafy vegetables*
* *Seaweeds*
* *Carrots*

FOLIC ACID

Folic acid works alongside vitamin 12 to form new cells, in particular those in our bone marrow which produce red and white blood cells. Research has suggested that it has a role to play in preventing birth defects such as spina bifida and pregnant women should increase their intake of folic acid rich foods.

GOOD SOURCES

* *Yeast extract*
* *Wheatgerm*
* *Nuts* – especially peanuts
* *Beans, peas & pulses*
* *Fortified breakfast cereals*
* *Green leafy vegetables* – especially spinach, broccoli, cabbage

Minerals

IRON

Iron is essential for the formation of red blood cells and the functioning of several enzymes in the body.

GOOD SOURCES

* *Tofu*
* *Beans & pulses*
* *Nuts & seeds*
* *Green leafy vegetables*
* *Dried fruits* – apricots, prunes
* *Blackstrap molasses*
* *Wheat germ and wholemeal cereals*

CALCIUM

Calcium is essential for the growth and maintenance of bones and for controlling nerve impulses to and from the brain.

GOOD SOURCES

* *Tofu*
* *Dairy products*
* *Fortified soya products*
* *Green leafy vegetables* – especially watercress
* *Okra*
* *Nuts* – especially almonds & brazils
* *Dried fruits i.e. figs, apricots*

ZINC

Zinc is vital for the functioning of the body, especially the immune system and resistance to infection.

GOOD SOURCES

* *Dairy products*
* *Nuts & seeds i.e. pumpkin & sesame*
* *Wholegrains, cereals and rice*
* *Wheat germ*
* *Pulses* – lentils

IODINE

Essential for many metabolic functions especially the proper functioning of the thyroid gland.

GOOD SOURCES

* *Seaweeds*
* *Iodized salt*
* *Green leafy vegetables*

MAGNESIUM

Needed for normal calcium function. It is also used in every cell in our bodies and to enable some enzymes needed for energy to function properly.

GOOD SOURCES

* *Wholegrain cereals & wheatgerm*
* *Soya products*
* *Tofu*
* *Nuts & seeds*
* *Green leafy vegetables*
* *Dried fruits i.e. figs, prunes*

All the recipes in this book have been carefully tested to ensure that you get the right results but it is important to bear all of the following in mind before you begin.
(NB: Metric and imperial measurements are not interchangeable, so be sure to follow one or the other.)

Standard conversions

25g	1oz
50g	2oz
85g	3oz
115g	4oz
140g	5oz
175g	6oz
200g	7oz
225g	8oz
250g	9oz
275g	10oz
350g	12oz
400g	14oz
450g	1lb
700g	1lb 9oz
1kg	2lb 4oz

125ml	4fl oz
150ml	¼ pint
300ml	½ pint
450ml	¾ pint
600ml	1 pint
900ml	1½ pints
1 litre	1¾ pints
1.2 litres	2 pints
1.7 litres	3 pints
2.25 litres	4 pints

Ovens are all slightly different, so you may need to adjust the temperatures given in the recipes accordingly or use an oven thermometer for the most accurate reading. Fan-assisted ovens can cook food faster than conventional ovens. To compensate, you can reduce the temperature given in a recipe, but it is best to consult the manufacturer's handbook. Fan-assisted ovens have an even temperature throughout, but in conventional ovens the heat rises, so the top of the oven is hotter than the bottom. When a dish is cooked in the oven, always use the middle shelf.

140°C	275°F	gas 1	very slow
150°C	300°F	gas 2	very slow
160°C	325°F	gas 3	slow
180°C	350°F	gas 4	moderate
190°C	375°F	gas 5	moderate
200°C	400°F	gas 6	moderately hot
220°C	425°F	gas 7	hot
230°C	450°F	gas 8	hot
240°C	475°F	gas 9	very hot

Equipment

Buy the best tools and equipment you can afford, as it will last better and will produce better results.

- *Kitchen scales*
- *Measuring jug:* 600ml/1 pint jug with metric and imperial
- *Metric measuring spoons:* 1.25ml (¼ tsp), 2.5ml (½ tsp), 5ml (1 tsp) and 15ml (1 tbsp)

Pots and pans

A heavy base is particularly important for gentle, even heat distribution. They also need to have lids that fit tightly and sturdy handles that stay cool.

- *Saucepans:* 1 litre/small, 2 litre/medium and 3 litre/large capacity with lids
- *Non-stick frying pans:* 20cm/8 inches and 30cm/12 inches or 35cm/14 inches in diameter, preferably with lids
- *Casserole:* large, heavy and flameproof, preferably cast iron coated in enamel, with a lid
- *Wok:* single, long handle and a lid
- *Steamer:* a double saucepan – the top or inner pan having holes which allows the steam to permeate around the food
- *Omelette pan:* 18cm/7 inches or 20cm/8 inches in diameter with curved sides
- *Crêpe pan:* with flat bottom and shallow, sloping side
- *Milk pan:* small, non-stick, with spout for pouring
- *Stockpot:* large, tall and narrow
- *Stove-top grill pan:* ridged base

Knives

- *Chef's or cook's knife:* rigid, heavy, wide blade 20cm/8 inches or 25cm/10 inches long
- *Sharp knife for cutting fruit and vegetables:* blade 12cm/5 inches or 15cm/6 inches
- *Small knife for trimming and peeling:* blade 7cm/3 inches or 10cm/4 inches
- *Cutting boards*

Ovenware

It is a good idea to choose attractive dishes which can double as serving dishes.

- *Roasting tin*
- *Flat baking trays*
- *Loaf tins:* 450g/1lb and 900g/2lb
- *Cake tin:* deep, loose-bottomed 18cm/7 inches or 23cm/9 inches in diameter
- *Springform cake tin:* the sides open out and the bottom is loose to allow easy removal
- *Soufflé dishes or ramekins:* for individual servings
- *Sandwich tins:* 2 x 18cm/7 inches for layered cakes
- *Swiss roll tin:* with shallow sides, usually 23 x 33cm/9 x 13 inches
- *Tartlet tins (individual)*
- *Large gratin dish*
- *Oval or round pie dish*

STARTERS

Crispy Vegetable Wontons ᵥ *China*

Wontons are an oriental version of the Italian ravioli. They are made using very thin wrappings or skins, which are made from wheat flour paste. They are sold ready-made in Asian shops and can be stored in the refrigerator for up to five days or frozen successfully. (If you do freeze them, make sure that they are thoroughly defrosted before use.) Filo pastry makes a good alternative.

Preparation time:
30 minutes

Cooking time:
15 minutes

SERVES 4 (MAKES APPROXIMATELY 20 WONTONS)

1 tbsp groundnut oil
50g/2oz carrots, finely grated
115g/4oz cabbage, finely grated
50g/2oz beansprouts
2 large cloves garlic, chopped finely
1 tbsp soy sauce
3 tbsp mashed tofu, or low-fat vegetarian soft cheese
pinch each of sea salt and unrefined sugar

1 tsp sesame oil
½ tsp black pepper
20 wonton skins or 275g/10oz filo pastry
vegetable oil for deep-frying
1 quantity Sweet and Sour Chilli Dipping Sauce (page 146) or Garlic Dipping Sauce (page 147)

Heat a wok or large frying pan and add the oil. When it is hot, stir-fry the carrots, cabbage, beansprouts and garlic for 1 minute. Set the vegetables aside and allow them to cool.

After they have cooled, combine the vegetables with the rest of the ingredients. Put a generous teaspoonful of the filling in the centre of each wonton skin. Pull up two opposite corners, dampen the edges with a little water and pinch them together. (If you are using filo pastry, cut a double thickness into 10-cm/4-inch squares, and brush lightly with water before filling them.) Bring up the other two corners, pinch them together with the first two, and seal with a little water, so that they look like small bundles.

Pour 5–7.5cm/2–3 inches of oil into a medium saucepan and place on a medium to high heat. The oil is ready when a cube of bread browns immediately. Deep-fry the wontons in several batches until they are golden and crisp. Drain them on kitchen paper. Serve at once, with the Sweet and Sour Chilli Dipping Sauce (page 146) or the Garlic Dipping Sauce (page 147).

PEELING GARLIC

Press down on the clove with the flat side of a knife blade, then pull away the burst skin.

Crispy Vegetable Wontons

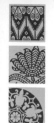

Sichuan Fried Aubergines with Spicy Sauce ~ *China*

The cuisine of the Sichuan province in central China has been popular in the West for many years. It is associated with the spicy flavours of Sichuan peppercorns and dried red chillies, and typically uses salt, garlic and ginger, soy sauce, fiery bean paste and fermented pickled vegetables.

Preparation time:
25 minutes

Cooking time:
15 minutes

SERVES 4–6

115g/4oz plain flour
1 tsp baking powder
¼ tsp sea salt
1 large free-range egg
2 tbsp olive oil
150ml/¼ pint water
3 tbsp chopped spring onions
1 tbsp finely grated fresh ginger
2 tsp chilli bean sauce, available from
　East Asian grocers

150ml/¼ pint vegetable stock (page 32)
1 tbsp rice or cider vinegar
2 medium tomatoes, skinned and
　chopped
3 tbsp tomato purée
2 tbsp soy sauce
groundnut oil for deep-frying
450g/1lb aubergines, cut into slices
　2.5 x 7.5cm (1 x 3 inches) and
　7.5mm/⅓ inch thick

For the batter, sift the flour with the baking powder and salt in a small bowl. Beat in the egg, then 1 tablespoon of olive oil, and finally the water. Beat until smooth. Leave the batter to stand for 20 minutes before using it.

Heat a wok or large frying pan and add the remaining tablespoon of olive oil. When the oil is hot, put in the spring onions, ginger and chilli bean sauce, and stir-fry for 1 minute. Add the stock, vinegar, chopped tomatoes, tomato purée and soy sauce and cook for a further minute. Set the sauce aside.

Pour 5–7.5cm/2–3 inches of oil into a medium saucepan and place on a medium to high heat. The oil is ready when a cube of bread browns immediately. Dip the aubergine slices in the batter and deep-fry them in several batches, turning them until they are golden all over. Remove the slices with a slotted spoon and drain them on kitchen paper. Keep them warm in a moderate oven while cooking the rest. Arrange the aubergines on a warm plate, and serve them hot, with the sauce in a small dish to hand around separately.

Savoury Puff Pastry Rolls ~ *UK*

These rolls are great as a starter, snack or cut smaller for a finger buffet. Kids love them so why not make plenty, freeze them and bake straight from frozen.

Preparation time:
15 minutes

Cooking time:
50 minutes

SERVES 4 (MAKES APPROXIMATELY 15 ROLLS)

2 tbsp olive oil
3 medium onions, chopped
4 vegetarian burgers (225g/8oz), broken into pieces
85g/3oz chopped mixed nuts
2 tbsp tomato purée

1 tbsp each freshly chopped sage and basil
sea salt and black pepper to taste
225g/8oz ready-made puff pastry
1 free-range egg yolk or a little dairy or soya milk to glaze

Heat the oil in a medium saucepan, add the onions and cover the pan with a lid. Soften the onions over a gentle heat for about 15 minutes, stirring occasionally, until they are translucent. Add the burger pieces and cook for a further 3–4 minutes. Remove the burger and onions from the pan and put them into a bowl with the nuts, tomato purée, herbs and salt and pepper to taste. Mix the ingredients thoroughly and allow the mixture to cool.

Roll the puff pastry into a rectangle 38 x 30cm/15 x 12 inches and cut it into three strips, each 12.5cm/5 inches wide. Form a third of the filling into a sausage along the centre of each strip, leaving a 2.5-cm/1-inch border on each side. Brush the top border with water and fold over the bottom border to cover the filling. Fold the top border over the bottom and secure the edges by pressing them in firmly.

Cut the pastry rolls into five even lengths and transfer them to a baking tray with the join underneath. Using a sharp knife, make three shallow cuts on the top of each one, brush with beaten egg yolk or a little milk and bake at 200°C/400°F/gas 6 for about 25 minutes or until the rolls have risen and turned golden brown.

SPARE EGG WHITES

Left-over egg whites can be easily frozen in small containers. They must be thoroughly defrosted in the fridge before use.

Asparagus Crêpes with Tarragon and Crème Fraîche ~ *France*

These elegant crêpes make a delicate starter for a special meal, and look very beautiful on the plate.

SERVES 6

Preparation time:
30 minutes
(plus 2 hours
standing time)

BATTER

140g/5oz plain flour, sifted
2 large free-range eggs
300ml/½ pint dairy or soya milk
150ml/¼ pint water
1 tsp vegetable oil, plus extra oil for frying
pinch of sea salt

FILLING

36 small, fresh asparagus spears, trimmed
2–3 tbsp freshly chopped tarragon
200ml/7fl oz crème fraîche
1 tsp freshly squeezed lemon juice
1 tsp unrefined caster sugar
black pepper to taste

For the batter, put the flour, eggs, milk, water, oil and salt into the blender, and run it for 1 minute. Alternatively, sift the flour into a medium bowl, add the eggs and slowly whisk in the milk, water, oil and salt to make a smooth batter. Leave it to stand for 2 hours.

Heat a 18-cm/7-inch frying pan until hot, then moisten it with a small amount of oil. Carefully pour in 2 tablespoons of the batter and swirl it around the base of the pan to form a thin pancake. Cook the crêpe until it is golden and crisp on both sides. Remove it from the pan and keep it warm in a moderate oven between sheets of foil or greaseproof paper while you make the other crêpes. Repeat the steps until you have made twelve crêpes in all. Brush the pan lightly with a little more oil if necessary between crêpes, and regulate the temperature of the pan to prevent them from burning.

Cook the asparagus until tender, standing it in boiling water so that the tips steam above the surface and the base of the asparagus is soft. This will take about 6–7 minutes. Drain the asparagus thoroughly; allow it to cool slightly before laying three spears in the middle of each pancake.

Mix the chopped tarragon into the crème fraîche and season with the lemon juice, sugar and pepper to taste.

Spoon a little of the sauce over the warm asparagus, fold both sides of the crêpe over the centre so that the asparagus protrudes at each end and serve at once with the remaining sauce on the side.

TIP

When asparagus is out of season, you can replace it with 450g/1lb leeks, washed, trimmed and sliced across. The leeks will take longer to boil and need to be drained thoroughly, but leek crêpes make an equally splendid starter.

Asparagus Crêpes with Tarragon and Crème Fraîche

Broccoli and Parmesan Tartlets ~ *France*

A classic French starter, these individual tartlets also make a super light lunch. Serve them with the Fennel and Rocket Salad on page 50.

SERVES 6

350g/12oz Easy Shortcrust Pastry
  (page 153) or Crunchy Wholemeal
  Pastry (page 154)
½ large red onion, chopped finely
450g/1lb broccoli, steamed and cut
  into small florets

50g/2oz grated vegetarian Parmesan
4 large free-range eggs
125ml/4fl oz half-fat crème fraîche or
  soya cream
1 tsp ground cumin
black pepper to taste

Roll out the pastry thinly. Butter six 10-cm/4-inch fluted flan tins with removable bases, and line them with the pastry. Bake them blind (page 161) and allow them to cool.

Scatter the chopped red onion on top of the pastry. Fill the tins with the broccoli and scatter half of the Parmesan over the top.

Beat the eggs with the crème fraîche or soya cream and season with cumin and pepper. Pour the egg mixture over the broccoli. Sprinkle the top with the rest of the Parmesan.

Bake at 190°C/375°F/gas 5 for 25–30 minutes or until the pastry is crisp and the mixture has set in the centre. Cool on a rack for 5 minutes, then remove the tartlets from the tins.

Preparation time:
30 minutes

Cooking time:
25–30 minutes

PARMESAN
Parmesan cheese is traditionally made using animal rennet. However, there are now a few brands of Parmesan available with vegetable agents. If you cannot find one, substitute any finely grated mature, hard, vegetarian cheese.

Avocado Hummus v *Lebanon*

If, like me, you love traditional hummus, try this variation for a change. It is particularly good in a sandwich with chopped tomatoes, peppers and red onion.

SERVES 6–8

225g/8oz tinned chickpeas, drained
1 tbsp tahini paste
juice of 1 lemon
4 tbsp plain dairy or soya yoghurt
3 tbsp olive oil

1 clove garlic, crushed
2 large ripe avocados, peeled and stoned
sea salt and black pepper to taste
freshly chopped parsley to garnish

Place the chickpeas in the blender with the main ingredients up to and including the avocados. Blend until well mixed and smooth. Season to taste with salt and pepper, adding more lemon juice if necessary.

Put the hummus into a serving bowl, cover and chill in the fridge. Sprinkle with finely chopped parsley just before serving.

Preparation time:
10 minutes

TIP
Add a couple of chopped fresh spinach leaves to enhance the colour.

Caponata (AUBERGINE AND OLIVE SAUCE) v *Italy*

Preparation time:
1 hour

This classic Sicilian dish is delicious hot or cold, and is often enjoyed with grissini (bread sticks) or toasted bread as part of an antipasto. It sets off grilled vegetables beautifully and makes a delicious topping for pasta, pizza or grilled polenta slices.

SERVES 4–6

10 tbsp olive oil
1 large red onion, finely chopped
1 tsp tomato purée
2 tbsp balsamic vinegar
1–2 tbsp unrefined demerara sugar
400g/14oz tinned tomatoes with their
  juices, chopped

115g/4oz green olives, chopped
2 tbsp capers, finely chopped
2 medium aubergines, finely chopped
sea salt and black pepper to taste

Heat 2 tablespoons of the oil in a large pan, add the onion and cook over a medium heat for 10 minutes, until soft. Add the tomato purée and cook for 1 minute, then add the vinegar, sugar, tomatoes, olives and capers. Cook over a medium heat for a further 20 minutes.

In a medium frying pan, fry the aubergines in two batches, using 4 tablespoons of oil for each batch, tossing and turning them for about 10 minutes until they are soft and lightly coloured. Add the first batch to the tomato mixture before cooking the second.

Finally, mix everything together well, season to taste with salt and pepper, then allow the caponata to cool in a bowl. Check the seasoning again when it is cold, since the flavours mellow.

Pinto Bean Dip v *Mexico*

Preparation time:
10 minutes

When I visited the American South-west, I had my first taste of Mexican food and it soon became one of my favourites. Now the whole family loves it and it's a real winner. It is packed with protein, as beans and corn feature predominately in most dishes.

SERVES 4–6

400g/14oz tinned pinto beans, drained
1 tbsp olive oil, plus a little extra
juice of 1 lemon or 2 limes
1 medium red onion, chopped
1 tbsp coriander (or flat-leaf parsley if
  preferred)

1 clove garlic
½ each green and red chilli, de-seeded
  and chopped, to garnish

Blend all the ingredients until smooth. Put the dip into a serving dish, sprinkle it with the chopped chillies and drizzle a little olive oil over the top. Serve with tortilla chips or fresh vegetable sticks.

Chilli Corn Fritters ~ *Thailand*

These crisp, golden sweetcorn fritters, spiked with chilli and coriander, show clearly why Thai cuisine has become so popular in the West in recent years: they are irresistibly mouth-watering.

SERVES 3–4 (MAKES APPROXIMATELY 20 FRITTERS)

450g/1lb frozen or tinned sweetcorn kernels, defrosted (if appropriate) and drained
115g/4oz plain flour, sifted
2 tsp chilli powder
¼ tsp of coriander seeds, crushed
¼ tsp black pepper
2 tbsp chopped fresh coriander (or flat-leaf parsley if preferred)
1 small clove garlic, chopped
1-cm/½-inch piece fresh ginger, chopped
pinch of sea salt
1–2 tsp soy sauce to taste
1 large or 2 small free-range eggs, beaten
vegetable oil for shallow-frying
1 quantity Garlic Dipping Sauce (page 147)

Combine the corn with the other ingredients (apart from the oil) in a medium bowl and mix well. Pour 5mm/¼ inch of vegetable oil into a large frying pan and heat it until a little of the batter dropped into the oil sizzles immediately. Place 1 tablespoon of the batter at a time into the oil. Keep the fritters apart in the pan and fry until they are golden brown on both sides, about 4–5 minutes for each side. Repeat until all the batter has been used.

Drain the fritters on kitchen paper and keep them warm in a moderate oven until you have cooked them all and are ready to serve.

Preparation time:
10 minutes

Cooking time:
25 minutes

TIP
Instead of using chilli powder in the fritters use 1–2 fresh de-seeded and chopped red or green chillies with a pinch of cumin seeds, or 1 tsp red chilli flakes, and a pinch of cumin seeds.

Melizanasalata (AUBERGINE DIP) V *Greece*

This keeps for days, covered, in the fridge. Serve at room temperature, drizzled with a little olive oil and garnished with chopped parsley and black olives. Serve with warmed pitta bread.

SERVES 4–6

450g/1lb aubergines
1 small red onion, sliced finely
1 large clove garlic, crushed
60ml/2fl oz olive oil
juice of ½ lemon
sea salt and black pepper to taste
chopped parsley and a few halved olives to garnish (see above)

Prick the aubergines with a fork and bake them at 180°C/350°F/gas 4 for 40–45 minutes, turning once or twice.

Leave them to cool, then peel them and chop the flesh, allowing the juices to run off. Put the flesh into the blender with the onion, garlic, olive oil, lemon, salt and pepper and blend well. Put the dip into a bowl and chill in the fridge.

Preparation time:
1 hour

Chilli Corn Fritters with Garlic Dipping Sauce

Fried Courgettes and Aubergines **v** *Greece*

Arrange the courgettes and aubergines on a plate and place it in the centre of the table, where everyone can help themselves. They are best served immediately.

Preparation time:
25 minutes

SERVES 4

2 medium courgettes, washed and cut in
  quarters lengthwise and halved
  crosswise
1 large aubergine, trimmed and sliced
  into 1-cm/½-inch rounds
plain flour to coat

vegetable oil for shallow-frying
sea salt and black pepper to taste
lemon quarters to garnish
1 quantity Skorthalia Sauce
  (page 147)

TIP
Use the freshest courgettes with unblemished skin. They will turn slightly bitter if they are not used within a few days of purchase. Likewise, the aubergine needs to be fresh, with a smooth, deep purple skin.

Sift the flour on to a large plate and roll the prepared courgettes and aubergines in it until they are well coated.

Heat 5mm/¼-inch of oil in a large frying pan until it is hot. Add the courgettes and cook until they are golden brown, turning occasionally – they will take about 8 minutes, and will need to be cooked in batches. Remove them with a slotted spoon and drain them on kitchen paper. Keep them warm in a moderate oven.

Using fresh oil, fry the aubergine slices a few at a time until they are golden brown on both sides, removing and draining them as before. Keep them warm, and repeat until all the slices have been cooked.

Arrange the fried courgettes and aubergines on a warm plate and sprinkle them with salt and pepper to taste. Place lemon wedges around the edge of the plate, and serve with the Greek thick garlic sauce called skorthalia.

Fried Courgettes and
Aubergines with Skorthalia
Sauce

Curried Sweetcorn V *India*

An unusual way of serving sweetcorn, this dish makes the most of classic Indian flavours. Serve it with a traditional Indian bread such as naan or chapati.

SERVES 4

4 tbsp vegetable oil
450g/1lb frozen or tinned sweetcorn, or kernels freshly cut from the cob
1 large onion, chopped finely
4 tbsp freshly chopped coriander (or flat-leaf parsley if preferred)
2 cloves garlic, crushed

2.5-cm/1-inch piece fresh ginger, peeled and grated
2 tsp ground cumin
2 tsp curry powder
150ml/¼ pint plain dairy or soya yoghurt

Heat the oil in a large frying pan or wok and fry the corn for about 3 minutes over a medium heat, turning until the kernels are lightly browned. Using a slotted spoon, remove the corn from the pan.

Add the onion to the pan and fry until it is soft, about 10 minutes, then add the coriander or parsley, garlic and ginger. Stir well for 2 minutes, then add the spices. Simmer for 8–10 minutes, remove from the heat and stir in the yoghurt just before serving.

Preparation time:
35 minutes

TIP

When sweetcorn is in season, use fresh kernels cut off the cob. To do this, hold the cob vertical and run a sharp knife down behind the kernels to remove them from the cob. Cut in strips until all the kernels have been removed.

Chile Con Queso V *Mexico*

Vegetarian mince can be used straight from the freezer. If you defrost it first remember to adjust the cooking time accordingly.

SERVES 6–8

2 tbsp olive oil
1 red onion, chopped finely
175g/6oz frozen vegetarian mince
4 anaheim or jalapeño chillies (page 123), de-seeded and chopped
3 medium tinned plum tomatoes, drained and chopped

150ml/¼ pint single dairy or warmed soya cream
450g/1lb low-fat vegetarian cream cheese or soft soya 'cheese'
sea salt to taste
freshly chopped coriander (or flat-leaf parsley if preferred), to garnish

Heat the oil in a large frying pan, add the onion and cover the pan with a lid. Soften the onion over a gentle heat for about 10 minutes, stirring occasionally. Add the mince and cook, stirring, for 5 minutes. Add the chillies and tomatoes, and simmer without a lid for about 10 minutes.

Mix the cream into the cream cheese and beat until smooth. Add to the pan and stir over a medium heat until hot. Season to taste. Allow the chilli to cool slightly before serving.

Garnish with chopped coriander or parsley, and serve with warm tortilla pieces or tortilla chips on the side.

Preparation time:
40 minutes

Felafels v *Lebanon*

Preparation time:
30 minutes
(plus
chilling time)

Egyptian in origin, these West Lebanese felafels take some beating. Try serving them in pitta bread with a combination of chopped spring onion, tomato, radish, cucumber, lettuce, white cabbage and pickled chilli, dressed with Yoghurt with Fresh Mint or Tahini Citrus Sauce (page 147).

S E R V E S 4 (M A K E S A P P R O X I M A T E L Y 2 0 F E L A F E L S)

2 x 400g/14oz tin chickpeas, drained
1 tsp each ground cumin, turmeric
    and sea salt
1 clove garlic, crushed
50g/2oz fresh breadcrumbs
3 tbsp freshly chopped coriander (or
    flat-leaf parsley if preferred)

2 tbsp water
plain flour to coat
vegetable oil for deep-frying
1 quantity sauce (see above)

Put the chickpeas, spices, garlic, breadcrumbs and preferred herb into a food processor. Process until the chickpeas are finely chopped but not puréed. Put the mixture into a large bowl and add the water. Knead the mixture and then, with floured hands, shape into twenty walnut-sized balls, slightly flattening each one. Chill them in the fridge for at least 30 minutes.

  Pour 5–7.5cm/2–3 inches of oil into a medium saucepan and place on a medium to high heat. The oil is ready when a cube of bread browns immediately. Roll the felafels in flour and deep-fry them in several batches until they are browned all over, about 2–3 minutes on each side, turning once. Drain on kitchen paper before serving.

Black-eyed Bean Cakes ~ *Africa*

Preparation time:
30 minutes

These fabulous bean cakes used to be cooked in markets throughout Africa centuries ago, but are almost a thing of the past – so now is the time to revive them!

S E R V E S 3 – 4 (M A K E S 1 2 B E A N C A K E S)

400g/14oz tinned black-eyed beans,
    drained
1 medium onion, chopped finely
1 tbsp freshly chopped coriander (or
    flat-leaf parsley if preferred)
½ tsp each allspice, cumin, cayenne
2 tbsp breadcrumbs

2 large free-range egg yolks
sea salt and black pepper to taste
2 tbsp each flour and sesame seeds
vegetable oil for shallow-frying
1 quantity Chunky Tomato Sauce with
    Harissa (page 146)

Combine the beans, onion, coriander or parsley, spices, breadcrumbs and egg yolks in the blender until smooth. Season to taste with salt and pepper.

  Roll tablespoons of the mixture in flour and coat them with sesame seeds. Heat 5mm/¼ inch of oil in a large frying pan until it is hot. Fry the bean cakes for 3–4 minutes on each side, until they are well browned. Drain on kitchen paper and serve them warm with the chunky tomato sauce.

Spring Rolls ∨ *Vietnam*

These Vietnamese-style spring rolls are an interesting variation of the more commonly known Chinese spring roll. Serve them with the Ginger Dipping Sauce.

SERVES 4–6 (MAKES APPROXIMATELY 20–24 SMALL SPRING ROLLS)

50g/2oz bean thread vermicelli, soaked in warm water for 5 minutes
50g/2oz carrots, grated finely
85g/3oz mangetout, sliced finely
3 tbsp finely sliced spring onions
2 tsp dark sesame oil
1 tsp rice wine vinegar
2 tbsp soy sauce
paprika to taste

1 packet rice papers, or spring roll wrappers, available from East Asian grocers (or filo pastry cut into squares 12.5 x 12.5cm/5 x 5 inches)
groundnut oil for deep-frying
sprigs of mint, washed and dried
small crisp lettuce leaves to garnish, such as little gem, washed and dried
1 quantity Ginger Dipping Sauce (page 146)

Preparation time:
35 minutes

Cooking time:
35 minutes

Drain the vermicelli and chop it roughly into 7.5-cm/3-inch lengths. In a medium bowl, mix the noodles with the carrots, mangetout, spring onions, sesame oil, vinegar and soy sauce. Season to taste with paprika.

If you are using rice papers, fill a large bowl with warm water and dip them into it one at a time to soften. Dry them on a clean tea towel, and put 1 tablespoon of the filling in the middle of the paper. Fold in each side, then roll it up tightly. Repeat until you have used up all the filling.

Pour 5–7.5cm/2–3 inches of oil into a medium saucepan and place on a medium to high heat. The oil is ready when a cube of bread browns immediately. Deep-fry the spring rolls a few at a time until they are golden brown all over. Drain them on kitchen paper and allow them to cool slightly.

TIP

When serving, place a dish of crisp lettuce leaves and sprigs of fresh mint on the table. Before eating each roll, place a small mint leaf on to a lettuce leaf and wrap this around the spring roll.

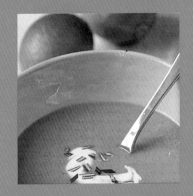

SOUPS

Vegetable Stock v

Homemade stock is the best, but if you are in a hurry a vegetable stock cube is a good option.

Preparation time: 25 minutes

MAKES 2.25 LITRES/4 PINTS

1 leek	6 peppercorns
2 onions	1 bay leaf, a few parsley stalks and a
3 carrots	few sprigs of thyme
4 celery sticks	2 litres/3½ pints water
5 cloves garlic	sea salt to taste

Peel and clean all the vegetables, and chop them coarsely. Put them into a large saucepan with the rest of the ingredients and bring to the boil. Turn down the heat and simmer for 20 minutes. Remove the pan from the heat and leave the stock to cool completely. Strain and chill it in the fridge.

TIP

Use up cooking water left from steaming vegetables both in stock and in gravy (page 149) for extra flavour.

Plantain and Corn Soup v *Africa*

Plantains are a kind of cooking banana, which is firmer and starchier than regular bananas. They are best cooked and eaten as a vegetable. If you can't find plantains, squash or pumpkin also work well.

Preparation time: 25 minutes

SERVES 4

2 tbsp vegetable oil	1.2 litres/2 pints vegetable stock
1 onion, chopped finely	(see above)
1 clove garlic, crushed	1 green chilli, de-seeded and
275g/10oz yellow (half-ripe)	chopped finely
plantains, peeled and sliced	pinch of grated nutmeg
1 large tomato, skinned and chopped	sea salt and black pepper to taste
175g/6oz sweetcorn kernels (fresh	4 sprigs of fresh tarragon to garnish
or frozen)	
1 tsp dried or 2 tsp freshly chopped	
tarragon	

Heat the oil in a large saucepan and add the onion and garlic. Fry for 5–6 minutes over a medium heat until the onion is soft.

Add the plantains, tomato and sweetcorn and cook for 5 minutes, stirring.

Add the tarragon, stock, chilli, nutmeg and salt and pepper to taste. Simmer for 10–15 minutes or until the plantain is tender.

Serve in individual bowls, garnished with a sprig of fresh tarragon.

TIP

Plantains are not that easy to peel. For slices, cut the plantain across at intervals and soak the pieces in salted water for about 30 minutes or until you can ease the pieces out of the skin. Keep the pieces in the salted water until you need them to prevent them discolouring. For strips, cut down the length of the plantain, not too deeply but just enough so that you can use a small knife to help pry off the skin.

Tom Yum Soup v *Thailand*

This light soup demonstrates the characteristic flavours of Thai cooking – lemon grass, chilli and coconut.

Preparation time:
30 minutes

SERVES 6

850ml/1½ pints vegetable stock (page 32)
400ml/14fl oz tinned coconut milk
3 tbsp freshly chopped coriander (optional)
2 tbsp groundnut oil
2 tbsp finely chopped garlic
1 medium onion, chopped finely
1 fresh chilli, de-seeded and chopped finely

2 stalks lemon grass
350g/12oz aubergine, cut into 1-cm/½-inch cubes
225g/8oz tinned chopped tomatoes
2 tsp unrefined sugar
sea salt and white pepper to taste
85g/3oz cooked basmati or Thai jasmine rice
6 tbsp finely chopped roasted or raw peanuts to garnish

TIP

If you can't find tinned coconut milk, you can make your own by pouring hot milk (or boiling water) over desiccated coconut in a bowl or jug, and allowing it to stand for 20 minutes before straining it.

In a medium saucepan, bring the stock and coconut milk to a simmer. For a more Asian flavour, add a small handful of fresh coriander to the stock.

Heat a wok or large frying pan and add the oil. When it is hot, add the garlic, onion, chilli and lemon grass, and stir-fry over a high heat for 2 minutes, then add the aubergine and cook for about 4 minutes until it has browned. Stir in the tomatoes and sugar, and mix well.

Add the vegetables to the stock, season to taste with salt and pepper and simmer for about 5 minutes. Add the rice 2 minutes before the end of the cooking time.

Remove the lemon grass, and pour the soup into individual bowls. Garnish with chopped peanuts.

Cucumber, Quark and Dill Soup ~ *Germany*

This soup is simple to make and brings out the light summery flavours of cucumber and fresh dill. Quark is a German low-fat soft cheese made from skimmed milk, and is high in protein. A good low-calorie alternative to cream cheese, it can be eaten on its own or used as an ingredient for cooking.

Preparation time:
10 minutes (plus
chilling time)

SERVES 4

400g/14oz quark
3 tbsp lemon juice
2 tbsp freshly chopped dill
600ml/1 pint vegetable stock (page 32)

1 large cucumber, peeled and coarsely grated
sea salt and black pepper to taste
4 sprigs of fresh dill to garnish

In a large bowl, mash together the quark, lemon juice, dill and stock, and stir until smooth. Mix in the grated cucumber.

Chill the soup in the fridge for a minimum of 1 hour, then season with salt and pepper to taste and serve garnished with dill.

Hot and Sour Soup v *China*

You'll find variations of this soup all over East Asia, where the philosophy of cooking focuses on health and well-being.

Preparation time:
1 hour 10 minutes

SERVES 4

2 tbsp cornflour blended with 5 tbsp water

4 tbsp rice or white wine vinegar

3 tbsp water

1 tbsp dry sherry

2 tbsp light soy sauce

black pepper to taste

2 tbsp vegetable oil

3 slices fresh ginger, shredded finely

1 medium onion, sliced finely

40g/1½oz shiitake mushrooms, shredded

425ml/¾ pint water

15g/½oz Chinese or porcini dried

mushrooms, soaked in hot water for 20 minutes, then drained and sliced

85g/3oz tinned straw mushrooms, halved

85g/3oz tinned bamboo shoots, cut into matchstick strips

2 spring onions, shredded

1 green or red chilli, sliced lengthwise and de-seeded

600ml/1 pint vegetable stock (see tip below)

115g/4oz frozen peas, defrosted

chopped spring onions to garnish

Mix the cornflour, vinegar, water, sherry and soy sauce together until smooth. Season to taste with pepper.

Heat the oil in a wok or large frying pan over a medium heat and stir-fry the ginger, onion and shiitake mushrooms for 2 minutes. Add the water, bring it to the boil and add the dried mushrooms, straw mushrooms, bamboo shoots, spring onions, chilli and stock.

Bring to the boil and simmer gently for 30 minutes, then add the peas and heat them through. Cook gently for 3 minutes, then slowly stir in the vinegar mixture until the soup thickens.

Remove the chilli and garnish with chopped spring onions before serving.

TIP

Save the water from the dried mushrooms to use for the stock and top it up with vegetable stock (page 32) to make 600ml/1 pint.

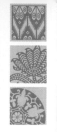

Broccoli and Stilton Soup ~ *UK*

Stilton is unique to three specific counties in the East Midlands of England: Leicestershire, Nottinghamshire and Derbyshire, and the traditional recipe cannot officially be made anywhere else in the world.

Preparation time:
35 minutes

SERVES 4–6

50g/2oz butter or margarine
1 small red onion, chopped
450g/1lb broccoli, chopped roughly
3 tbsp wholemeal flour
1.2 litres/2 pints vegetable stock
  (page 32)

5–6 spinach leaves, washed (optional)
40g/1½oz vegetarian Stilton cheese,
  crumbled
black pepper to taste
pinch of chilli powder (optional)

Heat the butter or margarine in a large saucepan, add the onion, cover and cook over a medium heat. Soften the onion for 5 minutes, stirring occasionally. Add the broccoli and toss it with the onion for a further 5 minutes until it is tender.

Sprinkle on the flour and toss again until it is thoroughly incorporated. Add the stock, stirring all the time. Bring the soup to simmering point and cook gently, covered, for 10 minutes or until the broccoli is completely soft. Stir in the spinach leaves for the last 2 minutes to enhance the colour, if you wish.

Remove the pan from the heat, purée the soup in the blender and put it back in the pan. Return the pan to the heat and stir in the crumbled cheese until it melts. Season to taste with pepper and a little chilli powder.

GARNISHES FOR SOUP

An attractive and well thought out garnish can make all the difference to a soup. Fresh herbs are a popular choice and they should be chosen to enhance or lift the flavour of the soup itself. Other effective garnishes are grated or crumbled cheese, vegetarian bacon bits, toasted nuts, croûtons, chopped spring onion or diced cucumber. Always add your chosen garnish at the last moment. I like to add a swirl of soya cream, crème fraîche or olive oil as it always adds an attractive finishing touch.

Green Jade Soup V *China*

A delicate soup from China, this is a simple combination of spinach and sweetcorn lightly flavoured with soy sauce.

Preparation time:
20 minutes

SERVES 4–6

225g/8oz cooked or frozen leaf
   spinach, thawed (450g/1lb fresh)
200g/7oz tinned sweetcorn, drained
   and blended roughly
2 tsp cornflour mixed with 2 tbsp water

850ml/1½ pints vegetable stock (page
   32)
2 tbsp soy sauce
black pepper to taste
4 spring onions, white part only

TIP

Cut a deep cross into the leaf end of the spring onions and leave them to soak in cold or iced water in the fridge until they open like flowers.

Put the spinach and sweetcorn into a large saucepan and heat them to a simmer for about 4–5 minutes. Stir in the cornflour and water mixture to thicken the juices released by the vegetables.

Gradually add the stock, stirring all the time. Add the soy sauce and mix it in well, then season to taste with pepper. Simmer the soup for 2 minutes.

Serve at once, garnishing each portion with a spring onion flower (see tip).

French Onion Soup V *France*

This soup was made famous at Les Halles when it was the market area in Paris.

Preparation time:
1 hour

SERVES 6

4 tbsp vegetable oil
1kg/2lb 4oz white onions, sliced thinly
1 tsp unrefined sugar
1.7 litres/3 pints vegetable stock
   (page 32)
150ml/¼ pint dry red wine

sea salt and black pepper to taste
12 slices French bread
3 cloves garlic, halved
225g/8oz vegetarian Gruyère, grated
   (omit for vegans)

In a large heavy saucepan, heat the oil and add the onions. Cook gently, stirring, over a medium heat until they are covered with oil, then reduce the heat and cover the pan. Cook for 30 minutes until the onions are soft and brown, stirring occasionally.

Add the sugar and pour in the vegetable stock and wine. Simmer for 20 minutes and season to taste with salt and pepper.

Pre-heat the grill. Just before the soup is ready, toast the slices of bread on both sides then rub them with the cut cloves of garlic. Ladle the soup into six ovenproof soup bowls and put two slices of the toasted bread on top of each serving.

Sprinkle the grated cheese on the bread and place the bowls under the grill until the cheese melts and bubbles and begins to brown. Serve at once.

Vegetable Soup with Coconut ▼ *Africa*

A combination of turnip, sweet potato and pumpkin, laced with silky coconut and fired by chilli, this soup is as full of contrasts as the African continent itself.

Preparation time: 50–55 minutes

SERVES 4

2 tbsp vegetable oil
1 large onion, chopped
175g/6oz each turnip, sweet potato and pumpkin, peeled and cubed
1 tsp dried marjoram
1½ tsp each ground ginger and cinnamon
sea salt and black pepper to taste
1 tbsp chopped spring onion

1.2 litres/2 pints vegetable stock (page 32)
2 tbsp flaked almonds
1 fresh chilli, de-seeded and chopped
1 tsp unrefined sugar
115g/4oz creamed coconut
freshly chopped coriander (or flat-leaf parsley if preferred), to garnish

In a large saucepan heat the oil, add the onion and cook it gently for 4–5 minutes. Add the cubed vegetables and toss them over a medium heat for a further 5–6 minutes.

Add the marjoram, ginger, cinnamon, salt and pepper and cook together over a low heat for 10 minutes, stirring frequently.

Add the spring onion, stock, flaked almonds, chilli and sugar and simmer gently for 10–15 minutes until the vegetables are just tender. Check the seasoning.

Grate the creamed coconut into the soup and stir well. Sprinkle with chopped coriander or parsley and serve.

Scotch Broth ▼ *Scotland*

In Scotland this hearty soup is sometimes referred to as 'barley broth'. The leek and root vegetables are traditional ingredients.

Preparation time: 1 hour 30 minutes

SERVES 6–8

3.4 litres/6 pints vegetable stock (page 32)
175g/6oz pearl barley
2 medium carrots, peeled and sliced
1 white turnip or 125g/4oz swede, peeled and diced
1 leek, cleaned and cut into thin slices

2 sticks celery, trimmed and sliced thinly
1 large onion, chopped small
175g/6oz Savoy or green cabbage, sliced into narrow ribbons
175g/6oz frozen peas, defrosted
sea salt and black pepper to taste

In a stockpot, heat the stock and add the barley. Bring to the boil, cover and simmer for 45 minutes.

Add the remaining ingredients to the pot (apart from the peas) and bring it to the boil again. Simmer gently, covered, for 30 minutes or until the barley is cooked. Add the peas for the last 7–8 minutes.

Season to taste with salt and pepper, and serve in large soup bowls.

Vegetable Soup with Coconut

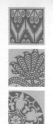

Spicy Lentil Soup with Sausages v *Germany*

This lentil soup is a complete meal in a bowl. It is lovely served with thick wedges of granary bread, or it can be made into a more substantial meal by serving it with Dumplings (page 152).

Preparation time:
45 minutes

SERVES 4–6

2 tbsp olive oil
2 medium onions, chopped finely
2 large carrots, chopped
4 sticks celery, chopped finely
1 dried red chilli pepper (optional)
2 cloves garlic, crushed
1 tsp ground coriander
1 tsp ground cumin

225g/8oz red lentils
1.4 litres/2½ pints vegetable stock
  (page 32)
150ml/¼ pint tomato juice
8 vegetarian sausages, grilled
sea salt and black pepper to taste
chopped parsley to garnish

Heat the oil in a large saucepan. Add the chopped onion, carrots and celery, and chilli if using, and cook over a low heat for 5 minutes, stirring occasionally.

Stir in the garlic and spices. Cook for a further minute or two, then stir in the lentils. Gradually stir in the stock and the tomato juice. Cover and simmer for about 20 minutes until the vegetables are tender.

Cut the grilled sausages into thick slices. Remove the soup from the heat and stir in the sausage slices. Season to taste with salt and pepper.

Serve sprinkled with chopped parsley.

Ravioli and Spinach Broth v *Italy*

The success of this soup relies on the vegetable stock, so use one with lots of rich flavour, such as that on page 32.

Preparation time:
25 minutes

SERVES 4

1.7 litres/3 pints vegetable stock
16 small or 8 large fresh ravioli with
  your favourite vegetarian filling
225g/8oz baby spinach leaves, washed

sea salt and black pepper to taste
2 tbsp freshly chopped parsley to
  garnish
grated vegetarian Parmesan (optional)

In a large saucepan, heat the stock to simmering point and add the ravioli (check the cooking time on the packet). As soon as it floats to the top, stir in the spinach and simmer gently for a further 2 minutes.

Season to taste with salt and pepper, ladle the soup into bowls and sprinkle parsley over the top. Serve at once, with grated Parmesan (omit this for vegans).

Spicy Lentil Soup
with Sausages

Chilled Red Pepper and Lime Soup ᴠ *France*

This stunning soup is incredibly quick to make considering the sophisticated result.

Preparation time:
5 minutes

SERVES 4

2 medium fresh red peppers, grilled and
   skinned or 225g/8oz tinned
juice of 2 limes
2 tbsp olive oil
400g/14oz tinned chopped tomatoes
75ml/2½fl oz low-fat crème fraîche or
   soya cream

1 tsp unrefined sugar
½ tsp cayenne pepper
iced water to thin
crème fraîche or soya cream and fresh
   rosemary, chopped, to garnish
sea salt and black pepper to taste

Put the peppers into the blender with the lime juice, olive oil and chopped tomatoes and blend to a smooth purée. Stir in the crème fraîche or soya cream and add the sugar and cayenne. Mix well, then chill in the fridge for at least 2 hours.

   Stir well and thin to a pouring consistency with iced water. Season to taste and garnish each bowl with a swirl of crème fraîche or soya cream and a little fresh rosemary before serving.

Black Bean Soup ᴠ *Mexico*

Black beans (*frijoles negro*) are kidney-shaped beans native to South America and are traditionally used in stews and soups.

Preparation time:
1 hour 30 minutes
(plus soaking time)

SERVES 4-6

115g/4oz black beans, soaked for a
   minimum of 8 hours
2 tbsp vegetable oil
1 medium onion, chopped
2 cloves garlic, sliced
1–2 green chillies, de-seeded and
   chopped
1.2 litres/2 pints vegetable stock
   (page 32)

2 tbsp tomato purée
1 bay leaf
300ml/½ pint soya milk, warmed
4 tbsp chopped coriander (or flat-leaf
   parsley if preferred)
sea salt and black pepper to taste

Drain and rinse the beans thoroughly. In a large saucepan heat the oil over medium heat and cook the onion, garlic and chillies, stirring occasionally until softened, about 5 minutes.

   Add the beans, stock, tomato purée and bay leaf and bring to the boil. Boil for 10 minutes, then reduce the heat, cover and simmer for a further 50 minutes, or until the beans are tender. Remove the bay leaf and purée the mixture in a liquidiser until smooth.

   Return to the saucepan then stir in the soya milk and re-heat gently. Stir in the coriander or parsley just before serving and season to taste.

*Chilled Red Pepper and
Lime Soup*

Pasta and Fava Bean Soup v *Italy*

Preparation time:
1 hour 30 minutes

This Italian mixture of pasta and fava beans makes a nourishing meal, served with warm Italian bread. If you don't have time to soak the beans, use tinned ones instead – they are just as good, but remember to halve the cooking time.

SERVES 6–8

5 tbsp olive oil
2 cloves garlic, chopped small
2 large carrots, peeled and diced
1 large onion, cubed
2 sticks celery, trimmed and diced small
400g/14oz tinned chopped tomatoes
1.5 litres/2¾ pints vegetable stock
  (page 32)

250g/9oz fava or cannellini beans,
  soaked for a minimum of 8 hours
4 tbsp freshly chopped parsley
1 tbsp freshly chopped oregano,
  rosemary or thyme
1 bay leaf
140g/5oz macaroni or any small pasta
sea salt and black pepper to taste

Heat the oil in a stockpot over a medium heat. Add the garlic, carrots, onion and celery and sauté for 5 minutes. Then add the chopped tomatoes, stock, fava beans, parsley, oregano or other herbs and the bay leaf. Bring to the boil, boil rapidly for 10 minutes, then reduce the heat, cover and simmer for 40–50 minutes until the beans are just tender.

Add the macaroni and cook for a further 10 minutes, so that it becomes soft and well cooked. Season to taste with salt and pepper.

Tomato and Rosemary Soup v *USA*

Preparation time:
10 minutes

Tomato soup has always been a family favourite. This recipe, with its hint of rosemary, is light, creamy and refreshing, and especially good in the summer when tomatoes are at their best.

SERVES 4

40g/1½oz margarine, or 2½ tbsp
  vegetable oil
15g/½oz plain flour
150ml/¼ pint soya cream
150ml/¼ pint soya milk

1 quantity Tomato Coulis (page 150),
  warmed
sea salt and black pepper to taste
2 sprigs of rosemary

In a medium saucepan, melt the margarine or heat the oil over a gentle heat and stir in the flour. Add the soya cream slowly, stirring all the time, until smooth. Then slowly stir in the soya milk and add a sprig of rosemary.

Stir in the tomato coulis slowly, so that the soup does not separate. Simmer very gently for 2 minutes.

Season to taste with salt and pepper, then serve garnished with rosemary.

Pasta and Fava Bean Soup

Minted Pea and Spinach Soup v *UK*

This soup is beautiful in colour and flavour. It can be served, either hot or chilled, with croûtons.

Preparation time:
30 minutes

SERVES 4–6

25g/1oz butter or margarine
1 large onion, chopped
450g/1lb fresh spinach, washed
225g/8oz frozen peas, defrosted
850ml/1½ pints vegetable stock
 (page 32)

3 tbsp freshly chopped mint
150ml/¼ pint low-fat crème fraîche,
 or warmed soya cream, plus extra
 to garnish
fresh mint leaves to garnish
1 quantity Croûtons (page 152)

In a large saucepan, heat the butter or margarine over a medium heat, add the onion and cook until it softens, about 5 minutes.

Shred the spinach, add it to the pan and stir until it wilts. Add the peas and stir again. Gradually add half of the stock, stirring, and bring it to the boil. Simmer for 5 minutes, stirring occasionally.

Purée the soup in the blender. Return it to the pan, add the chopped mint and stir for a further 2 minutes, then add the rest of the stock and heat it through.

Remove the pan from the heat, stir in the crème fraîche or soya cream, and reheat the soup gently. Serve garnished with fresh mint leaves and crème fraîche or soya cream.

Cream of Broccoli and Squash Soup v *USA*

A smooth, blended soup, this is wonderful food for cold weather. I sometimes use pumpkin instead of squash. Serve sprinkled with chopped chives.

Preparation time:
40–45 minutes

SERVES 6–8

4 tbsp olive oil
1 medium onion, diced
2 medium cloves garlic, crushed
700g/1lb 9oz broccoli, chopped
450g/1lb squash or pumpkin, peeled
 and chopped
1 large bay leaf
1 tsp sea salt

1.2 litres/2 pints vegetable stock
 (page 32)
600ml/1 pint single dairy or warmed
 soya cream
½ tsp each dried marjoram, thyme and
 basil
black pepper to taste
freshly chopped chives to garnish

In a stockpot, heat the oil, add the onion and garlic and cook over a low heat until translucent, about 10 minutes. Add the broccoli, squash or pumpkin, bay leaf, salt and stock. Cover and simmer for 15–20 minutes until the vegetables are tender. Blend until smooth.

Return the soup to the pan and stir in the cream. Add the dried herbs and season to taste with pepper. Simmer gently for a further 10 minutes before serving.

Minted Pea and Spinach Soup
with Croûtons

Watercress and Potato Soup v *France*

This is very simple to make and full of minerals and vitamins.

Preparation time:
30 minutes

SERVES 6

450g/1lb potatoes, peeled and chopped
1 medium onion, chopped
850ml/1½ pints vegetable stock (page 32)
300ml/½ pint skimmed dairy or warmed soya milk

2 bunches watercress, trimmed and chopped finely
large pinch of ground nutmeg
sea salt and black pepper to taste

In a large saucepan, simmer the potatoes and the onion in the stock until tender, about 20 minutes. Blend to a smooth purée.

Stir in the milk and add the chopped watercress. Simmer for 2–3 minutes, then season to taste with nutmeg, salt and pepper.

TIP

You can prepare the potato and onion base in advance and reheat it when you add the milk and watercress.

Green Minestrone v *Italy*

A great classic of Italian cuisine, minestrone never fails to be popular. This recipe, using all green vegetables with fresh summer herbs, is light and delicate.

Preparation time:
1 hour 30 minutes

SERVES 8

3 tbsp olive oil
2 cloves garlic, crushed
4–5 spring onions, chopped finely
4 sticks celery, sliced finely
225g/8oz broccoli, cut into florets
225g/8oz green beans, cut into short lengths
175g/6oz frozen peas
175g/6oz cabbage, shredded finely
medium bunch of parsley, chopped finely

2.25 litres/4 pints vegetable stock (page 32)
175g/6oz very small pasta shapes
3–4 tbsp mixed freshly chopped herbs (such as basil, oregano, marjoram or thyme)
sea salt and black pepper to taste
freshly grated vegetarian Parmesan (optional)

In a large stockpot, heat the oil, add the garlic, spring onions and celery, and cook over a medium heat for 5 minutes.

Add the rest of the vegetables and the parsley, and stir for 2 minutes. Gradually add the stock. Bring it to the boil and simmer, covered, for 30 minutes. Remove from the heat and stir in the pasta.

Leave the soup to stand, uncovered, for 15 minutes, until the pasta is soft, then stir in the chopped herbs and season to taste with salt and pepper.

Serve hot, with grated Parmesan (omit this for vegans).

TIP

Minestrone is even tastier the day after it is made, when the flavours have developed.

SALADS

Lettuce Hearts with Avocado, Croûtons and Blue Cheese Dressing ~ *USA*

I discovered this wonderful salad while visiting the West Coast of America and enjoyed it so much that I decided to include it here. I often make it when friends come for lunch.

Preparation time:
15 minutes

SERVES 4

Croûtons (page 152), using 4 slices of
    granary bread
40g/1½oz vegetarian blue cheese
Classic Vinaigrette (page 151)
2 tbsp soured cream, or crème fraîche

3 little gem or sweetheart lettuces
2 medium ripe avocado, peeled and
    stoned
black pepper to taste
finely chopped chives to garnish

Prepare the croûtons.

   Crumble the cheese and mix it thoroughly into the vinaigrette until smooth. Add the soured cream or crème fraîche and season with black pepper.

   Remove any bruised outer leaves of the lettuces. Cut lengthwise into quarters, rinse and pat dry. Slice the avocado thinly. Put three segments of lettuce on each plate with some slices of avocado. Spoon the dressing over the top. Scatter with the croûtons and finish with black pepper and a sprinkling of chives.

Fennel and Rocket Salad **v** *Italy*

Lovely and simple, this salad is hard to beat. It is perfect for a light summer lunch.

Preparation time:
10 minutes

SERVES 6

3 large fennel bulbs
350g/12oz rocket leaves, washed and
    dried
75ml/2½fl oz olive oil
1 tbsp balsamic vinegar

sea salt and black pepper to taste
40g/1½oz vegetarian Parmesan (or any
    mature, hard, vegetarian cheese),
    shaved finely (optional)

Trim the fennel and remove the outside layer. Cut the bulbs into quarters and slice the quarters into thin crescents. Combine the fennel with the rocket in a salad bowl.

   Mix the olive oil with the vinegar and season to taste. Toss the salad with the dressing, check the seasoning and lay the shaved cheese over the top before serving; omit the cheese for vegans.

TIP

You can buy a packet of seeds and grow rocket on your windowsill as you would herbs. It is easy to grow and far less expensive than buying it at the shop.

Lettuce Hearts with Avocado, Croûtons and Blue Cheese Dressing

Crispy Rice Noodle and Tofu Salad v *China*

A salad as attractive as this one also makes a wonderful starter. The crispy noodles, firm tofu and crunchy beansprouts are invigorated by the tangy dressing.

Preparation time:
25 minutes

SERVES 4

groundnut oil for deep-frying
115g/4oz rice vermicelli
175g/6oz firm tofu, cut into 1-cm/
   ½-inch cubes
115g/4oz beansprouts
3 spring onions, chopped finely
1 fresh chilli, de-seeded and chopped
4 tbsp chopped coriander (or flat-leaf
   parsley if preferred)

1–2 cloves garlic, crushed, to taste
3 tbsp yellow bean sauce
1 tbsp unrefined sugar
3 tbsp cider vinegar
4 sprigs of fresh coriander (or flat-leaf
   parsley if preferred) to garnish

Pour 5–7.5cm/2–3 inches of oil into a medium saucepan and place on a medium to high heat. The oil is ready when a cube of bread browns immediately. Deep-fry the noodles briefly, in several batches, until they puff up. Remove them with a slotted spoon and drain them well on kitchen paper.

Deep-fry the cubed tofu until golden, remove it with a slotted spoon and drain it on kitchen paper.

Divide the crispy noodles between four individual bowls and garnish them with the tofu, beansprouts, spring onions, chilli and chopped coriander or parsley.

Mix the garlic, yellow bean sauce, sugar and vinegar together. Pour the dressing over the salad just before serving, and garnish with coriander or parsley sprigs.

Cajun Rice Salad v *USA*

Peppers of every kind are crucial to Cajun cooking: this colourful salad uses red, yellow and green capsicums, as well as peppery spices. Make it as chilli-hot as you can stand to give this vigorous dish its authentic Cajun effect!

Preparation time:
30 minutes

SERVES 4–6

150g/5oz long-grain rice
40g/1½oz each chopped red and yellow
   pepper
25g/1oz tinned mild green chilli,
   chopped finely
40g/1½oz red onion, chopped finely

1–2 sticks celery, chopped finely
Creole Vinaigrette (page 151)
Tabasco to taste (optional)
4 spring onions, chopped finely
small bunch of parsley, chopped finely

Cook rice according to packet instructions. Combine the rice, peppers, chilli, red onion and celery in a salad bowl. Toss thoroughly with sufficient vinaigrette to moisten and season to taste with the optional Tabasco. Sprinkle with the chopped spring onions and parsley before serving.

*Crispy Rice Noodle and
Tofu Salad*

Louisiana Potato Salad v *USA*

A light spicing of Tabasco in this salad gives it its regional flavour, as Tabasco Pepper Sauce was originally created by the McIlhenny family of Louisiana in the 1860s.

SERVES 6

10 medium waxy potatoes, unpeeled
Classic Vinaigrette (page 151)
25g/1oz each red and green pepper,
  chopped finely
1 large stick celery

1 small red onion, chopped finely
sea salt and black pepper to taste
Tabasco to taste
3–4 spring onions, chopped finely
15g/½oz finely chopped parsley

Preparation time:
20 minutes
(plus 1 hour
marinating)

Cooking time:
20 minutes

Quarter the potatoes and place them in a large saucepan, cover with boiling water and cook until tender. Drain, allow them to cool slightly and then cut into slices 1-cm/½-inch thick. Place in a large bowl, toss with sufficient viniagrette to moisten and allow to marinate for at least 1 hour. Then mix in the chopped vegetables and season to taste with salt, pepper and Tabasco.

Garnish with the spring onions and parsley before serving.

Watercress Salad with Mushrooms and Gruyère ~ *Switzerland*

Gruyère is an excellent choice for this salad, as its firm texture and sweet, nutty flavour combine so well with the other ingredients.

SERVES 4

2 bunches of watercress, washed and
  trimmed
50g/2oz mushrooms, sliced thinly
1 tbsp freshly chopped thyme
115g/4oz vegetarian Gruyère cheese,
  grated

1 clove garlic, crushed
Classic Vinaigrette (page 151)
sea salt and black pepper to taste

Preparation time:
10 minutes

Combine the watercress, mushrooms and thyme in a large salad bowl, and toss with the grated cheese.

Mix the garlic into the vinaigrette and season to taste with salt and pepper. Toss with sufficient vinaigrette and serve immediately.

Cephalonian Salad ~ *Greece*

Preparation time:
15 minutes

This salad originates from the Greek island of Cephalonia. The addition of dill sets off the more traditional ingredients beautifully and the lemon dressing gives it a real zing.

SERVES 4

1 medium cos lettuce
4 tbsp freshly chopped dill or fennel
5–6 spring onions, shredded finely
1 green pepper, de-seeded and cut into thin strips
3 large ripe tomatoes, chopped

12–15 black olives, pitted
115g/4oz vegetarian feta cheese, cubed
4 tbsp extra-virgin olive oil
2 tbsp lemon juice
sea salt and black pepper to taste

TIP

To enhance the flavour of the tomatoes, sprinkle them with a little sea salt and leave them to marinate for a few minutes.

Discard any bruised outer leaves of the lettuce and shred the rest very finely by rolling them into cigar shapes and cutting them as thinly as possible. In a large bowl, mix the lettuce with the dill or fennel and the spring onions. Toss in the green pepper, tomatoes, olives and feta.

Mix the oil and lemon juice, and season to taste. Carefully fold the dressing into the salad just before serving.

Baby Spinach and Avocado with Mushrooms and 'Bacon' v *USA*

Preparation time:
25–30 minutes

This salad combination has become something of a modern classic, and this version using vegetarian bacon is even better than the original.

SERVES 4

1 large ripe avocado, peeled and stoned
6–8 spring onions, sliced finely
50g/2oz firm button mushrooms, sliced thinly
225g/8oz baby spinach leaves, washed and torn into medium strips

Classic Vinaigrette (page 151)
4 tbsp vegetarian bacon bits, or 4 vegetarian bacon slices, fried and chopped

Slice the avocado, place it in a large bowl with the spring onions, sliced mushrooms and spinach. Add sufficient vinaigrette and toss lightly. Sprinkle with the bacon pieces and serve immediately.

Artichoke, Goats' Cheese and Walnut Salad ~ *France*

Preparation time:
15 minutes

This salad is from the Perigord region in south-western France, which is famous for its walnuts. The subtle flavour of the oil enhances the other flavours of this salad wonderfully.

SERVES 4

115g/4oz French beans, trimmed
½ butternut lettuce, or batavia
bunch of watercress
400g/14oz tinned artichoke hearts, sliced (approximately 5)
115g/4oz vegetarian goats' cheese, crumbled or diced

40g/1½oz walnuts, toasted (page 70) and chopped small
3 tbsp walnut oil, or olive oil
1 tbsp tarragon vinegar
1 clove garlic, crushed
sea salt and black pepper to taste

Steam the beans lightly for 5–6 minutes until they are cooked but still slightly crisp. Plunge them into cold water to cool, and cut them into 5-cm/2-inch lengths.

Tear the lettuce into strips, break the watercress into short lengths and put them in a large bowl with the artichokes, cheese and walnuts.

Make the dressing with the oil, vinegar and garlic, and season to taste with salt and pepper. Pour over the salad, toss lightly and serve at once.

Surfers' Salad v *USA*

Preparation time:
15–20 minutes

My son James created this energizing salad on a surfing holiday. You could experiment with different flavoured oils in your vinaigrette (page 80).

SERVES 4

1 soft lettuce, such as butternut, washed and dried
50g/2oz baby spinach leaves, washed and dried
1 bunch of watercress and/or lambs' lettuce, washed and dried
115g/4oz beansprouts

115g/4oz carrots, peeled and grated or sliced finely
40g/1½oz alfalfa sprouts
handful of basil leaves, torn roughly
4 large spring onions, halved and sliced lengthwise
Classic Vinaigrette (page 151)

Combine the ingredients in a large salad bowl. Toss with sufficient vinaigrette and serve immediately.

Artichoke, Goats' Cheese and
Walnut Salad

Cannellini Bean Salad **v** *Greece*

Bean salads are characteristic of Greek home cooking. This one is deliciously spiked with lemon and onion, and garnished with black olives and fresh oregano.

Preparation time:
10 minutes

SERVES 2–4

400g/14oz tinned cannellini or haricot
  beans, drained
1 small red onion, sliced finely
3 tbsp freshly chopped parsley
4 tbsp olive oil
juice of ½ lemon

sea salt and black pepper to taste
12–16 black olives
2 hard-boiled eggs, chopped (optional)
fresh oregano, finely chopped, to
  garnish

In a medium bowl, whisk the olive oil with the lemon juice and seasonings. Stir in the beans, onions and parsley and toss well.

Garnish the salad with the olives and the chopped hard-boiled eggs (omit for vegans) and sprinkle with fresh oregano.

TIP

If you want to reduce the onion flavour in this or any other salad, run the cut onion under cold water, or marinate it in a little vinegar before using it.

Sweet and Sour Cucumber Salad **v** *Thailand*

One of my daughters introduced me to this lovely Oriental salad in which the light flavour of cucumber is perfectly enhanced by the sweet and sour sauce. Chopped peanuts add a nice crunch.

Preparation time:
10–15 minutes

SERVES 4

150ml/¼ pint distilled white vinegar
150ml/¼ pint water
115g/4oz unrefined sugar
large pinch of salt
1 large cucumber, peeled

3–4 tbsp freshly chopped coriander (or
  flat-leaf parsley if preferred)
½ small red onion, chopped
50g/2oz chopped salted peanuts

Mix the vinegar, water, sugar and salt in a small saucepan and bring to the boil, stirring to dissolve the sugar. Allow the mixture to reduce and thicken slightly, about 8–10 minutes: it should reduce by about half. Remove the pan from the heat and set aside the sauce to cool. Meanwhile, cut the cucumber lengthwise into quarters, then slice it thinly crosswise and put the pieces into a bowl.

Once the dressing has cooled, add it to the bowl with half of the chopped coriander or parsley and the onion. Stir the ingredients together well.

Just before serving, stir in the peanuts and garnish with the remaining coriander or parsley.

Cannellini Bean Salad

Seaweed and Cucumber Salad ▼ *Japan*

Seaweed is a great source of vitamins and minerals, and this salad is a delicious introduction to it. There are many different types: wakame is dark green, mild flavoured and more akin to a conventional green vegetable. It is sold dried or pickled and can be eaten in salads or soups.

Preparation time:
15 minutes

SERVES 4

25g/1oz dried wakame seaweed, shredded
1 medium cucumber, peeled
3 tbsp rice or white vinegar

2 tbsp unrefined caster sugar
1–2 tbsp light soy sauce
2–3 tbsp sesame seeds, toasted (see tip), to garnish

Soak the wakame in hot water until it is soft and has expanded, about 5 minutes, then drain it thoroughly. If you cannot find it already shredded, slice it very finely at this stage.

Halve the cucumber lengthwise, remove the seeds and slice the lengths thinly to make half-moon shapes.

Mix together the vinegar, sugar and soy sauce.

Combine the wakame and cucumber in a medium bowl, cover with the dressing and sprinkle the top with toasted sesame seeds.

TIP
To toast seeds, place the seeds in a small dry frying pan over medium heat. Stir until golden.

Nutty Wild Rice Salad with Citrus Dressing ▼ *USA*

This variation of the classic rice salad is distinguished by using wild rice. If you prefer you can use a combination of long-grain white and wild rice. Simply cook the two separately and combine.

Preparation time:
45–50 minutes

SERVES 4

175g/6oz wild rice
115g/4oz hazelnuts, toasted (page 70), chopped coarsely
6 sun-dried tomatoes, cut into thin strips
juice of ½ medium orange

juice of ½ lemon
1 small fennel bulb, cubed small
Classic Vinaigrette (page 151) made with garlic
sea salt to taste

In a large saucepan bring the rice to the boil in 1.35 litres/2¼ pints water. Simmer uncovered for 45–50 minutes until the grains are swollen and tender, then drain.

Mix the hazelnuts with the sun-dried tomatoes, orange and lemon juice and the fennel. Stir the mixture into the cooked rice and toss the salad with sufficient garlic vinaigrette to moisten. Season to taste.

Seaweed and Cucumber Salad

Creole Spinach and Hot Pepper Salad v *USA*

The deep colours of the spinach, tomatoes and red pepper mixed with the fiery
Creole-style dressing make this salad as vibrant as Southern life itself!

Preparation time:
20 minutes

SERVES 4–6

450g/1lb fresh baby spinach leaves,
   washed, dried, and the larger leaves
   torn into small pieces
1 red pepper, de-seeded and cut into
   thin strips

25g/1oz spring onions, chopped finely
12 cherry tomatoes, halved
Creole Vinaigrette (page 151)
175g/6oz Spicy Pecan Mix (page 152)

In a large salad bowl, mix the spinach, red pepper, spring onions and cherry tomatoes.
Toss the salad with sufficient vinaigrette to moisten and sprinkle with the pecans.

Warm Beetroot Salad with Crème Fraîche v *France*

Freshly cooked beetroot is a gourmet experience and serving it warm, as in this salad,
brings out the very best of its flavour. (As an alternative, you can make a cold version
of this salad – simply peel the raw beetroot, grate it and toss it in a bowl with all the
other ingredients.)

Preparation time:
10 minutes

Cooking time:
40 minutes

SERVES 4–6

4 medium beetroots, unpeeled
1 small red onion, or 3 spring onions,
   chopped finely
4 tbsp cider vinegar, or white wine
   vinegar
1 tbsp unrefined caster sugar (optional)
1 tsp French mustard

1 tbsp olive oil
1 tbsp freshly chopped parsley
sea salt and black pepper to taste
150ml/¼ pint low-fat crème fraîche or
   plain soya yoghurt
finely chopped parsley or chives to
   garnish

Wash the beetroot and bake it at 180°C/350°F/gas 4 until it is tender, about 40
minutes. Allow the beetroot to cool until it is just warm enough to handle, then peel
and grate it coarsely. Place the grated beetroot in a bowl and mix in the chopped
onion.

In a small bowl or jar, combine the vinegar, sugar, mustard, oil, parsley, salt and
pepper, and stir well.

Pour the dressing over the beetroot and mix well, then fold in the crème fraîche or
yoghurt. Garnish the salad with chopped parsley or chives.

Creole Spinach and
Hot Pepper Salad

Sicilian Bean and Potato Salad v *Italy*

Simple ingredients are enhanced by the piquant Sicilian flavours of this salad.

Preparation time:
30 minutes

SERVES 6

450/1lb new potatoes, unpeeled
450g/1lb French beans, steamed and
  cut into 2.5-cm/1-inch lengths
225g/8oz cooked or tinned haricot or
  cannellini beans

1 small red onion, chopped finely
50g/2oz black olives, pitted and sliced
1–2 tbsp capers
Classic Vinaigrette (page 151)
freshly chopped parsley to garnish

In a medium saucepan cook the potatoes in boiling water until tender. Allow to cool slightly and cut in half. Mix the potatoes, beans, onion, black olives and capers in a large bowl.

Pour sufficient vinaigrette over the salad to moisten and toss well. Sprinkle with parsley and serve.

Warm Puy Lentils on a Bed of Rocket v *France*

These lentils take their name from Le Puy in central France. They have a delicate flavour and keep their shape and colour when cooked. If you can't find Puy lentils, you can use brown or green lentils instead. This salad is equally good warm or cold, and is great for picnics.

Preparation time:
35 minutes

SERVES 4–6

115g/4oz Puy lentils, washed and
  drained
1 large onion, peeled and cut in half
2 cloves garlic, peeled and cut in half
2 bay leaves
5 tbsp mayonnaise
4 tbsp crème fraîche or plain soya
  yoghurt

3 spring onions, chopped finely
2 tbsp finely chopped parsley
sea salt and black pepper to taste
85g/4–6oz rocket leaves
½ lemon

In a medium saucepan cook the lentils with the onion, garlic and bay leaves in 600ml/1pint of water. Simmer for 20–25 minutes until the lentils are tender but still slightly nutty. Drain them, and rinse under cold water to cool them a little. Discard the onion, garlic and bay leaves.

Mix the mayonnaise with the crème fraîche or yoghurt, spring onions and parsley. Season to taste with salt and pepper. Fold this sauce into the warm lentils.

Divide the rocket between individual plates, squeeze a little lemon juice over the leaves and spoon the lentils on top.

Sicilian Bean and Potato Salad

Mooli Salad ~ *Japan*

Crisp mooli (Japanese white radish) makes a wonderful salad mixed with Chinese leaves and beansprouts. The slight sweetness of some added dates is lovely.

SERVES 4

1 medium mooli, coarsely grated
1 large carrot, grated
4 large Chinese leaves, shredded
175g/6oz beansprouts
4 dates, stoned and chopped finely
5 tbsp mayonnaise

1-cm/½-inch fresh ginger, peeled and grated finely
1 small clove garlic, crushed
soy sauce to taste
freshly chopped coriander (or flat-leaf parsley if preferred) to garnish

Combine the prepared salad ingredients in a large bowl.

Mix the mayonnaise with the ginger and garlic, and season to taste with soy sauce.

Fold the dressing into the salad and mix well, before garnishing with chopped coriander or parsley.

Preparation time: 15 minutes

TIP
Beansprouts are often quite soft when you buy them. To crisp them up soak in a bowl with iced water for 5 minutes and drain thoroughly before using.

Rocket and Alfalfa Salad **v** *Italy*

Rocket is a big favourite of mine and this salad is a great way of serving it.

SERVES 2–4

115g/4oz rocket leaves, washed and dried
50g/2oz alfalfa sprouts

Classic Vinaigrette (page 151) made with garlic

Mix the rocket and alfalfa sprouts together in a salad bowl. Add sufficient vinaigrette to moisten. Toss and serve at once.

Preparation time: 10 minutes

Warm Courgette Salad **v** *Greece*

If you love courgettes, you'll enjoy this way of serving them. The salad is particularly delicious with the Spanokopitta (page 106).

SERVES 4

3 young firm courgettes, sliced lengthwise, 3mm/⅛-inch
2 tbsp olive oil

1 tbsp lemon juice
2 tbsp dill or parsley, chopped
sea salt and black pepper to taste

Steam the sliced courgettes for 3–4 minutes, until tender. Allow them to cool slightly, then place the slices on a serving plate.

Whisk the oil with the lemon juice, dill or parsley and salt and pepper to taste.

Pour the dressing over the courgettes and serve at once.

Preparation time: 15 minutes

QUICK AND EASY MEALS

Pesto Genovese with Green Beans
and Potato ~ *Italy*

Fresh pesto has always been one of my favourite pasta sauces because it uses so much delicious basil. In the Italian region of Liguria, pasta is traditionally cooked with potato and green beans, and served with pesto.

Preparation time:
25 minutes

SERVES 4–6

6 small waxy new potatoes, unpeeled	cut into 5-cm/2-inch lengths
350g/12oz dried penne or fusilli	4 tbsp Pesto Sauce (page 148)
350g/12oz green beans, trimmed and	basil leaves to garnish

Boil the potatoes until tender but still firm, about 15 minutes. When they are cool enough to handle, cut them into small cubes.

Cook the pasta according to packet instructions.

Meanwhile, steam the beans until tender but still lightly crisp, about 5–6 minutes.

Mix the vegetables with the pasta and toss in the pesto. Garnish with basil and serve immediately, with warm ciabatta bread.

Spaghetti alla Putanesca **V** *Italy*

Approaching the port of Genoa, sailors claimed they were met by the pungent smell of garlic even before they could see land on the horizon! According to local folklore, the pasta took its name from the prostitutes of the city, who cooked this hearty combination of garlic, capers and olives.

Preparation time:
15 minutes

SERVES 4

350g/12oz dried spaghetti	20 black olives, pitted and chopped
3 tbsp olive oil	small
1 red chilli, de-seeded and chopped	2 tbsp capers, chopped finely
(optional)	4 tbsp freshly chopped parsley
2 large cloves garlic, sliced finely	black pepper to taste

Cook the spaghetti according to packet instructions.

Heat the olive oil in a large saucepan, add the chilli and garlic and cook over a medium heat for 2 minutes to soften the garlic.

Add the olives and capers, and stir for a further 2 minutes.

Add the drained spaghetti to the pan and toss it with the sauce, adding the parsley and black pepper before serving.

Pesto Genovese with Green
Beans and Potato

Peasant Pasta v *Italy*

This recipe is from my friend Alistair and has become a firm favourite with everyone who tries it. It is especially good with crusty warm bread, such as ciabatta and a green salad.

Preparation time:
15 minutes

SERVES 4

350g/12oz dried conciglie (large pasta shells)
8 tbsp olive oil
400g/14oz tinned butterbeans, drained
2 cloves garlic, sliced thinly

1 tsp freshly chopped rosemary
400g/14oz tinned artichoke hearts, drained, rinsed and cut into quarters
sea salt and black pepper to taste
grated vegetarian Parmesan (optional)

Cook the pasta according to packet instructions.

Heat the oil in a large frying pan. Fry the butterbeans, garlic and rosemary for about 5 minutes, stirring occasionally, until the beans are lightly browned.

Add the artichokes and heat through. Season to taste.

Toss the mixture into the hot, drained pasta and serve with grated Parmesan (omit the Parmesan for vegans).

One-pot Mushroom Risotto v *Italy*

This tasty, easy dish has the added bonus of keeping the washing-up to a minimum!

Preparation time:
25–30 minutes

SERVES 4

50g/2oz butter or margarine
2 medium onions, chopped
225g/8oz mushrooms, chopped
225g/8oz long-grain rice
600ml/1 pint vegetable stock (page 32)
sea salt and black pepper to taste

175g/4oz frozen peas
1 medium courgette, sliced thinly
50g/2oz pine kernels or cashew nuts, toasted (see below)
4 tbsp freshly chopped parsley, to garnish

In a large saucepan, melt the butter and sauté the onions and mushrooms for 5 minutes.

Add the rice and stir well. Add the stock and seasonings, and bring the mixture to a simmer. Reduce the heat, cover and cook gently for 10 minutes.

Lay the vegetables over the top of the rice and cover again. Leave to steam for a further 10 minutes. Add more water if it begins to dry out.

Stir well, sprinkle with the pine kernels or cashews and the parsley before serving.

TOASTING NUTS

To toast nuts, preheat the oven to 180°C/350°F/gas 4. Lay the nuts on a baking tray and cook in the centre of the oven for 15–20 minutes until lightly and evenly golden – timings will depend on the type and size of the nuts. Alternatively, place the nuts on a baking tray under a pre-heated grill or in a dry frying pan over a medium heat and brown them, turning the nuts frequently.

Aromatic Vegetable Stir-fry v *China*

Preparation time:
10 minutes

Cooking time:
7 minutes

Fast food can still be healthy food and this stir-fry is lovely served with the Special Fried Rice (page 142).

SERVES 4

2 tbsp groundnut oil
2-cm/½-inch fresh ginger, finely
  chopped
1 each red, yellow and green pepper,
  diced

115g/4oz tinned water chestnuts, sliced
  thinly
50g/2oz tinned bamboo shoots, sliced
50g/2oz mangetout, trimmed
soy sauce to taste

Heat the oil in a wok or frying pan and add the ginger. Stir-fry for about 30 seconds so that it flavours the oil. Add the peppers, stir-fry for a further minute, then add the water chestnuts and bamboo shoots. Stir-fry for a further minute, then add the mangetout and toss for another minute.

  Add the soy sauce and remove the wok from the heat. Serve at once.

Spicy Tofu v *Vietnam*

Preparation time:
12 minutes

Tofu (also known as beancurd) is a rich source of protein. Make sure you use firm and not the silken variety for this particular recipe.

SERVES 4

1 tbsp groundnut oil
1 tbsp finely grated fresh ginger
1 tbsp finely chopped garlic
1 tbsp chilli bean sauce
2 tsp yellow bean sauce
50ml/2fl oz vegetable stock (page 32)

2 tbsp rice wine, or dry sherry
1 tsp cornflour mixed with 2 tsp water
700g/1lb 9oz firm tofu, drained, patted
  dry and cut into 1-cm/½-inch cubes
sesame oil and finely chopped spring
  onions to garnish

Heat a wok over a high heat and add the oil. Stir-fry the ginger, garlic and sauces together for 1 minute.

  Add the stock and the rice wine and simmer gently for 2 minutes.

  Stir the blended cornflour into the mixture. When it has thickened slightly, add the tofu and stir gently. Cook very gently for 2–3 minutes, and serve drizzled with a little sesame oil and sprinkled with chopped spring onions. Serve with rice, noodles or in a sandwich.

Overleaf: Oriental Feast (see
Menu Planner on page 187)

Sweet and Sour Tofu v *Thailand*

Tofu is soya bean paste which has been pressed into block form. I love it and enjoy cooking with it. It is versatile, absorbs flavours well and adds substance to any vegetarian dish.

Preparation time:
30 minutes

SERVES 4–6

FOR THE SAUCE:

1 tbsp cornflour
3 tbsp plus 175ml/6fl oz vegetable
    stock (page 32)
2 tbsp white wine vinegar
3 tbsp unrefined sugar
1 tbsp tomato ketchup
2 tbsp light soy sauce
¼ tsp cayenne pepper
black pepper to taste
1 tbsp vegetable oil
1 large clove garlic, chopped finely
1-cm/½-inch fresh ginger, grated

vegetable oil for deep-frying
350g/12oz firm tofu, cut into 5-cm/
    2-inch rods
soy sauce
2 tbsp vegetable oil
4 carrots, shredded or cut into ribbons
    with a potato peeler
8 spring onions, shredded

Mix the cornflour with 3 tablespoons of the stock until smooth.

In a medium bowl, mix together the vinegar, remaining stock, sugar, ketchup, soy sauce, cayenne and black pepper.

Heat 1 tablespoon of oil gently in a small saucepan, and soften the garlic and ginger. Add the vinegar mixture to the pan and simmer for about 4 minutes. Stir in the cornflour mixture until the sauce thickens. Check the seasoning.

Pour 5–7.5cm/2–3 inches of oil into a medium saucepan and place on a medium to high heat. The oil is ready when a cube of bread browns immediately. Deep-fry the tofu in hot oil for about 5 minutes until it is golden all over, drain it on kitchen paper, transfer it to a serving dish and sprinkle it with soy sauce.

Heat the remaining oil in a wok and stir-fry the carrots and spring onions for about 1 minute until they are cooked but still crisp.

Mix the vegetables with the tofu, and pour the sauce over the top.

TIP
Tofu is now readily available in most shops. Look out for the ready-marinated and smoked varieties, both of which would work very well in this recipe.

Baked Portobello Mushrooms ~ *USA*

Preparation time:
20 minutes

Cooking time:
20 minutes

Portobello mushrooms have a great depth of flavour, a firm texture and their size makes them ideal for filling. A long-standing favourite in the States, they are now increasingly available on this side of the Atlantic.

SERVES 4

4 Portobello or large flat mushrooms, stems removed
4 tbsp olive oil
juice of 1 lemon
1 clove garlic, chopped
2 tsp dried thyme

450g/1lb spinach leaves, blanched and chopped, excess moisture squeezed out
225g/8oz vegetarian Camembert, Brie or 115g/4oz goats' cheese
sea salt and black pepper to taste

Place the mushrooms in a baking dish. Mix the olive oil, lemon juice, garlic and thyme together and spoon over the mushrooms.

Bake in the oven for 10 minutes at 180°C/350°F/gas 4.

Top with the spinach and cheese and season to taste with salt and pepper. Place under a preheated grill until the cheese has melted, for about 2-3 minutes.

Mozzarella in Carrozza ~ *Italy*

Preparation time:
30 minutes

An Italian obsession, these mozzarella 'sandwiches' are dipped in egg and fried until the outside is golden and the inside melts. Serve with a green salad.

SERVES 4

1 loaf of ciabatta, cut into 24 slices
350g/12oz mozzarella, sliced thinly
12 slices plum tomato, or 12 sun-dried tomatoes
sea salt and black pepper to taste

12 fresh basil leaves
4 large free-range eggs
1 tsp dried oregano, or mixed herbs
150ml/¼ pint milk
olive oil for shallow-frying

Cover 12 slices of bread with half the mozzarella. Place a thin tomato slice, or a sun-dried tomato, on top and season with salt and pepper. Top with a basil leaf. Cover with the remaining mozzarella, and put another slice of bread over the top to make a sandwich.

Beat the eggs with the dried herbs and the milk in a large shallow dish. Dip the sandwiches in the egg mixture, turning them once or twice.

Heat 5mm/¼-inch of oil in a large frying pan until it is hot. Fry the sandwiches in batches for 2–3 minutes until they are golden on both sides. Drain the sandwiches on kitchen paper and serve immediately.

Baked Portobello Mushrooms

Rice 'n' Beans v *Caribbean*

Chilli heat tempered with coconut milk is the essence of Caribbean cooking. This dish is lovely with a simple avocado and tomato salad, tossed in Classic Vinaigrette made with lime juice (page 151).

Preparation time:
40 minutes

SERVES 4

1 medium onion, chopped finely
2 tbsp olive oil
225g/8oz vegetarian burgers, cubed
1 small chilli, trimmed and de-seeded
3 tomatoes, chopped small

600ml/1 pint coconut milk
350g/12oz long-grain rice
225g/8oz tinned black-eyed or kidney
   beans, drained
sea salt and black pepper to taste

In a large saucepan, sauté the onion in the olive oil then add the burger cubes and toss until they are lightly browned.

Then add the remaining ingredients except the beans and stir well. Bring to the boil, cover and simmer for 10 minutes. Stir in the beans and cook for a further 10 minutes until the rice is tender, adding water if necessary. Season to taste.

Oriental Fritter ~ *China*

Although this dish is called a fritter, it is really more like a pancake in texture. Once you have got the hang of making these, try them with any combination of your favourite vegetables.

Preparation time:
25–30 minutes

SERVES 2

4 tbsp plain flour
½ tsp sea salt
8 tbsp water
115g/4oz tinned straw mushrooms, or
   tiny button mushrooms, sliced
1 large free-range egg, beaten lightly
85g/3oz beansprouts

2 spring onions, sliced crosswise
2 tbsp soy sauce
1 tsp unrefined sugar
2 tbsp vegetable oil
1 clove garlic, chopped finely
freshly chopped coriander (or flat-leaf
   parsley if preferred) to garnish

In a large bowl, sift the flour with the salt and stir in the water gradually to make a smooth batter. Add the mushrooms, egg, beansprouts, spring onions, soy sauce and sugar, and stir thoroughly into the batter.

Heat the oil in a medium frying pan and cook the garlic until golden over a medium heat. Pour the batter into the pan and allow it to spread. Fry until the underside is crisp and golden. Cut the fritter into four pieces, then turn them over and cook the other side until golden and crisp. Serve garnished with a few leaves of coriander or parsley.

Layered Pasta Bake ~ *Greece*

Preparation time:
20 minutes

Cooking time:
20–25 minutes

This is a lovely dish which my daughter Mary made for me one evening. It goes well with the Surfers' Salad (page 57).

SERVES 6

400g/14oz tinned chopped tomatoes
115g/4oz tomato purée
200ml/7fl oz water
2 tsp dried thyme, or 1 tsp fresh, chopped
2 cloves garlic, crushed
10 sun-dried tomatoes, chopped
200g/7oz vegetarian feta, diced

sea salt and black pepper to taste
350g/12oz dried pasta (fusilli or penne)
1 medium onion, chopped
3 medium courgettes, sliced
3 tbsp olive oil
50g/2oz vegetarian Cheddar, grated
chopped fresh basil to garnish

In a medium saucepan, simmer the tomatoes, tomato purée and water with the thyme, garlic and sun-dried tomatoes. When the sauce has reduced and thickened a little, after 8–10 minutes, add the feta. Season to taste.

Meanwhile, cook the pasta according to the packet instructions. Drain, and mix it thoroughly with the tomato sauce.

In a medium saucepan, sauté the onion and courgettes in the olive oil for 2–3 minutes.

Spread half of the pasta mixture into a large baking dish and layer the courgette mixture over the top. Cover with the rest of the pasta mixture.

Sprinkle with the Cheddar and bake at 180°C/350°F/gas 4 for 20–25 minutes. Serve hot, sprinkled with fresh basil.

Gnocchi with Pumpkin Sauce ▼ *Italy*

Preparation time:
20 minutes

Gnocchi are tasty little dumplings made from mashed potato or semolina flour. Most regions of Italy have their own variations.

SERVES 4

650g/1lb 7oz pumpkin, diced
300ml/½ pint dairy or soya milk
1 tbsp freshly chopped sage or oregano
125ml/4fl oz single dairy or soya cream
sea salt and black pepper to taste
2 x 400g/14oz packets of fresh gnocchi, cooked according to packet instructions

30g/1oz vegetarian Parmesan, finely grated (optional)
50g/2oz hazlenuts, toasted (page 70), chopped
fresh sage leaves to garnish

In a large saucepan, simmer the pumpkin in the milk with the herbs until tender, about 10 minutes. Add the cream and cook for 1 minute. Season with salt and pepper.

Toss the sauce with the cooked gnocchi, sprinkle with Parmesan and hazelnuts and garnish with sage leaves before serving. Omit the Parmesan for vegans.

Chickpea and Okra Stir-fry v *Africa*

This is a truly delicious dish that uses okra, a green vegetable, which is also known as ladies' fingers. If you can't buy okra, courgettes will work just as well.

Preparation time:
25–40 minutes

SERVES 4

2 tbsp vegetable oil
15g/½oz butter or margarine
1 large onion, chopped finely
1 clove garlic, crushed
3 tomatoes, chopped
1 green chilli, de-seeded and chopped
1-cm/½-inch fresh ginger, grated

450g/1lb okra, trimmed
1 tsp ground cumin
1 tbsp freshly chopped coriander (or
flat-leaf parsley if preferred)
400g/14oz tinned chickpeas, drained
sea salt and black pepper to taste

In a large frying pan or wok, heat the oil with the butter or margarine. Sauté the onion and garlic for 4–5 minutes until the onion has softened.

Add the tomatoes, chilli and ginger, and stir well, then add the okra, cumin and coriander or parsley. Cook over a medium heat, stirring frequently, then stir in the chickpeas and a little seasoning.

Cook gently for a few minutes longer for the chickpeas to heat through, then spoon into a bowl and serve immediately.

FLAVOURED OILS

It is very easy to make your own flavoured oils and they can be used for stir frying, for marinading tofu or vegetables, for salad dressings or for moistening bread when sandwich-making. Here are a few suggestions but do experiment with your own combinations.

Thai – take 3 sprigs of fresh coriander and 3 x 5-cm/2-inch stems of lemon grass, plus 2 dried red birdseye chillies. Put them into a clean glass jar or bottle and pour in 500ml/16fl oz of rapeseed oil or corn oil. Seal the bottle and leave in a cool, dark place for 2 weeks.

Mexican – place 3 small red birdseye chillies (with seeds) into a clean glass jar or bottle and pour in 500ml/16fl oz of sunflower oil. Seal and leave in a cool, dark place for 1 week.

Italian – add 3 sprigs of small fresh basil leaves and 2 cloves of peeled garlic in a clean glass jar or bottle. Pour in 500ml/16fl oz of extra-virgin olive oil in. Seal and leave in a cool, dark place for 2 weeks.

French – take 1 sprig of rosemary, 1 sprig of thyme, 1 bay leaf and 6 black peppercorns. Put them in a clean glass jar or bottle. Pour in 500ml/16fl oz of extra-virgin olive oil and leave in a cool, dark place for about 2 weeks.

Indian – heat 2 tablespoons of olive oil in a pan and add 1 clove of garlic, 1 teaspoon of coriander seeds, 1 teaspoon of cumin seeds, a 1-cm/½-inch piece of fresh ginger root, finely chopped, and 1 tablespoon of curry paste. Cook over a medium heat for about 1 minute. Add 250ml/8fl oz of olive oil and cook for another 30 seconds. Leave to cool, then transfer to a clean glass jar or bottle.

Chickpea and Okra Stir-fry

Sandwiches

With the stunning selection of breads from around the world now available, the humble sandwich has been transformed from everyday snack-food into something of a gourmet treat! The key to creating a successful sandwich is to experiment and not be afraid to try out new flavours and combinations. Always use the freshest bread available – it is a good idea to slice loaves and rolls on the day you buy them, bag them up and put them in the freezer until you need them. You don't have to use butter or margarine – instead try using flavoured oils (page 80), Pesto Sauce (page 148), sun-dried tomato paste, or a squeeze of lemon juice or mayonnaise. Here are a few of my favourite combinations to get you started!

Cold Sandwiches

* Mature vegetarian Cheddar and home-made coleslaw in pumpkin seed bread
* Grated carrot, mayonnaise, Dijon mustard and rocket leaves in a crusty white roll
* Vegetarian blue cheese with thinly sliced apple and apricot chutney in a poppy seed bagel
* Cottage cheese, thinly sliced red onion and cucumber with wholegrain mustard in a wholemeal pitta pocket
* Wholenut peanut butter with fruit jam or banana in a soft white finger roll
* Baby spinach leaves, sliced marinated artichokes, black olives and feta cheese in soda bread
* Cream cheese or mashed tofu with garlic powder and finely chopped tomatoes, parsley and capers in toasted granary bread
* Thinly sliced tomatoes, avocado, vegetarian mozzarella and pesto in ciabatta
* Feta, tomato, cucumber, black olives, chopped oregano and lemon juice in a granary bap
* Cooked asparagus mixed with vegetarian blue cheese in walnut bread
* Hummus with sliced pickled beetroot in pumpernickel
* Vegetarian ham slices with apple chutney, alfalfa sprouts and shredded lettuce rolled up in an Indian flatbread
* Goats' cheese with spiced fruit chutney in sunflower seed bread
* Vegetarian chicken slices with sandwich pickle, mayonnaise, sliced gherkins and lettuce in soft white sliced bread
* BLT – vegetarian bacon slices, lettuce and sliced tomato, with mayonnaise in toasted granary bread
* Traditional club sandwich – vegetarian ham and chicken slices, mayonnaise and lettuce layered between three slices of lightly toasted white bread and served with vegetable crisps on the side

Hot Sandwiches

* Croque monsieur – vegetarian ham slices and cheese in white bread, fried in a little hot olive oil and butter until golden brown on both sides
* Sautéd aubergine and onion flavoured with mixed herbs, spooned into a baguette, topped with grated cheese and grilled until bubbling
* Warm oven-roasted vegetables (page 105) with soft goats' cheese in focaccia
* Toasted bagel spread with hummus and topped with capers
* Traditional hotdog with a vegetarian frankfurter served in a split white hotdog bun and topped with fried onion, ketchup and yellow mustard
* Warmed vegetarian turkey slices with Cranberry Sauce (page 148).

Stir-fried Vegetables with Tofu and Quinoa **V** *Bolivia*

Stir-fries are a brilliant way of cooking a quick and healthy meal. My daughter Heather came up with this inventive combination, but you can vary the vegetables and use whatever is to hand or in season.

Preparation time:
40 minutes

SERVES 4–6

175g/6oz quinoa (see below)
6 tbsp groundnut oil
250g/9oz firm tofu, cubed
1 medium onion, finely chopped
2 large garlic cloves, chopped
2 medium carrots, peeled and grated
½ small cauliflower, cut into small
   florets, blanched
1 medium red pepper, de-seeded and
   sliced
1 large or 2 small leeks, sliced
2 sticks celery, chopped

½ small cabbage, shredded
1½ tbsp tamari
1 tsp unrefined muscovado sugar
1 tbsp fresh lemon juice
½ tsp ground cinnamon
½ tsp ground nutmeg
½ tsp ground cloves
1-cm/½-inch fresh ginger, grated
sea salt and black pepper to taste
50g/2oz sunflower seeds, toasted
   (page 60)

Rinse the quinoa and put in a large saucepan with double its volume of cold water. Bring to the boil and cook uncovered for 10–15 minutes.

In a large frying pan, heat 2 tablespoons of the oil and fry the tofu until golden all over. Drain on kitchen paper and set to one side.

Heat the remaining oil in a wok. Sauté the onion and garlic, then add the carrots, cauliflower and pepper. Stir-fry over a medium heat for 3–4 minutes then add the leeks, celery and cabbage. Stir in the tamari, sugar and lemon juice, spices and fresh ginger. Add the quinoa and continue cooking over a medium heat for a further 5 minutes stirring continuously. Season to taste with salt and pepper. Serve topped with the tofu and sunflower seeds. This is delicious with mango chutney.

QUINOA

Quinoa is something of a wonder-grain. It's an ancient crop which is now being rediscovered. It is particularly useful to vegetarians, as it provides more protein than any other grain. It is becoming increasingly available in health-food shops and well worth trying to find. If your local shop doesn't stock it, ask – they may order it in for you.

MAIN COURSES

Red Enchiladas ~ *Mexico*

These appetizing tortillas are rolled up around a filling of mince, cheese and chopped onion, and topped with tomato salsa.

Preparation time:
25 minutes

Cooking time:
10–15 minutes

MAKES 12 (6 SERVINGS)

300ml/½ pint Salsa (page 151)
150ml/¼ pint tomato purée
150ml/¼ pint water
½ tsp each ground cumin and dried oregano
225g/8oz vegetarian mince
12 large tortillas

vegetable oil for frying
225g/8oz vegetarian Cheddar, grated
1 large red onion, chopped finely
12 black olives, pitted and chopped
1 small iceberg lettuce, shredded
1 quantity Salsa Verde (page 150), (optional)

In a medium saucepan mix the salsa with the tomato purée, water, cumin and oregano, and bring to a boil. Reduce the heat and simmer for 15 minutes stirring occasionally.

Sauté the mince in 1 tablespoon of oil until lightly browned. Keep to one side. Then in a large frying pan lightly fry the tortillas in oil on one side for a few seconds only. Spread 4–6 tablespoons of the sauce over the bottom of a large ovenproof dish. Brush each tortilla with more of the sauce, then fill it with some of the cheese and mince, and ½ tablespoon of the chopped onions, and roll it into a tube. Place the tortilla seam-side down in the dish. Repeat with the other tortillas, reserving a little cheese and onion to garnish.

Spoon any remaining red sauce over the tortillas, and sprinkle them with the reserved cheese and onions and the olives. Bake at 180°F/350°F/gas 4 for 10–15 minutes. Serve at once, with the shredded lettuce and salsa verde if using.

Mung Bean Stew ᴠ *Kenya*

This is half-way between a soup and a stew, and is great served with plain boiled rice.

Preparation time:
1 hour
(plus soaking time)

SERVES 4

225g/8oz mung beans, soaked for a minimum of 8 hours
25g/1oz butter, margarine or ghee
2 cloves garlic, crushed
1 medium red onion, chopped
2 tbsp tomato purée

½ each green and red pepper, de-seeded and cut into small cubes
1 green chilli, de-seeded and chopped finely
300ml/½ pint water

Drain the mung beans and put them into a large saucepan. Cover the beans with water, and boil for 30–40 minutes until tender. Remove them from the heat: mash half with a fork or potato masher and leave the other half whole.

Heat the butter, margarine or ghee in a medium saucepan, add the garlic and onion and fry until golden brown. Add the tomato purée, the mashed beans, whole beans, then the peppers and chilli. Add the water, and mix well. Cover and simmer for about 20 minutes. Serve hot.

Red Enchiladas

MAIN COURSES

Sambhar (LENTIL CURRY WITH VEGETABLES) ∨ *India*

This great Indian dish is delicious and simple to make. The flavours develop well over twenty-four hours, so it is excellent kept and reheated.

Preparation time:
50 minutes

SERVES 4–6

225g/8oz red lentils, washed
1 tbsp curry powder
1 tsp ground turmeric
8–10 okra, trimmed
225g/8oz cauliflower florets
225g/8oz mooli (white radish), peeled
   and sliced thickly
1 medium onion, sliced thickly
2 tsp unrefined soft brown sugar
sea salt to taste

4 small tomatoes, quartered
1 red pepper, de-seeded and chopped
3 tbsp vegetable oil
½ tsp mustard seeds
2 whole dried chillies
½ tsp cumin seeds
2 green cardamom pods
2 cloves garlic, crushed
fresh coriander leaves (or flat-leaf
   parsley if preferred) to garnish

Place the lentils, curry powder and turmeric in a large saucepan with sufficient water to cover them, and bring to the boil. Simmer, covered, until the lentils are mushy – about 20 minutes. Be careful that they do not dry out, add more water if necessary.

Mash the lentils with a potato masher or wooden spoon and add the okra, cauliflower, mooli, onion and brown sugar. Add enough water to give the curry the consistency of a thick soup, and simmer again until the vegetables are tender, about 15–20 minutes. Season to taste with salt. Add the tomatoes and red pepper, cover and keep the curry warm.

In a small frying pan heat the oil and fry all the remaining spices and a little salt with the garlic until the mixture crackles. Pour this over the sambhar, and serve garnished with fresh coriander leaves or parsley.

COOKING WITH SPICES

Spices do not deteriorate as quickly as herbs do, but it is still a good idea to buy them whole where possible (i.e. nutmeg, black pepper) and grind them yourself as required, as this will make them last even longer. Whole spices can usually be kept for at least a year, and ground ones will keep for about six months. Always store your spices in airtight jars in a cool, dark, dry place – a spice rack on display in your kitchen may look attractive but will shorten their life considerably.

Spicy Peanut Noodles with
Satay Cauliflower and Broccoli v *Indonesia*

Satay is one of the great classic sauces of the Orient. These spicy noodles are served with steamed broccoli and cauliflower, but they are also excellent with courgettes.

SERVES 6

350g/12oz rice noodles
700g/1lb 9oz mixed cauliflower and
  broccoli florets
5 tbsp sesame oil
225g/8oz oriental mushrooms, such as
  shiitake or oyster
1 tbsp crunchy (wholenut) peanut butter
juice of ½ lime
1 tbsp yellow bean sauce

1–2 tbsp soy sauce to taste
1 large clove garlic, chopped finely
½ tsp chilli powder
6 spring onions, cut diagonally into
  1-cm/½-inch pieces
2 tbsp finely chopped peanuts
fresh coriander (or flat-leaf parsley if
  preferred) to garnish
1–2 quantities Satay Sauce (page 148)

In a large bowl soak the rice noodles in warm water according to packet instructions. Drain.

Meanwhile steam the cauliflower and broccoli florets until they are *al dente* for about 5 minutes. In a large frying pan heat 2 tablespoons of sesame oil over high heat and sauté the mushrooms for 1–2 minutes. Mix the peanut butter with the lime juice, the remaining sesame oil, yellow bean sauce, soy sauce, garlic and chilli powder. Toss the sauce into the drained noodles, then add the spring onions, mushrooms and peanuts and toss again. Pile onto a large serving plate. Top with the steamed vegetables and satay sauce and garnish with the fresh coriander or parsley.

Chickpea Roast ~ *India*

This was inspired by my love of Indian food. It goes really well with the Sambhar opposite and Curry Sauce (page 146).

SERVES 4–6

4 large sticks celery, chopped small
225g/8oz cauliflower, diced small
400g/14oz tinned chickpeas, drained
1 green pepper, de-seeded and
  diced small

15g/½oz brown breadcrumbs
1 tbsp soy sauce
1 tbsp curry powder, or 1–2 tbsp
  Indian curry paste to taste
1 large free-range egg, beaten

Steam the celery and cauliflower until tender, about 6–7 minutes. In a large bowl mash the chickpeas roughly. Add all the vegetables.

Stir in the breadcrumbs, add the soy sauce and curry powder to taste and bind with the egg. Place in a greased 23 x 12.5-cm/9 x 5-inch loaf tin.

Bake at 180°C/350°F/gas 4 for 45–50 minutes until set. Cool the roast on a rack for at least 20 minutes before turning it out. Cut into slices using a very sharp knife.

Red Enchiladas ~ *Mexico*

These appetizing tortillas are rolled up around a filling of mince, cheese and chopped onion, and topped with tomato salsa.

Preparation time:
25 minutes

Cooking time:
10–15 minutes

MAKES 12 (6 SERVINGS)

300ml/½ pint Salsa (page 151)
150ml/¼ pint tomato purée
150ml/¼ pint water
½ tsp each ground cumin and dried
   oregano
225g/8oz vegetarian mince
12 large tortillas

vegetable oil for frying
225g/8oz vegetarian Cheddar, grated
1 large red onion, chopped finely
12 black olives, pitted and chopped
1 small iceberg lettuce, shredded
1 quantity Salsa Verde (page 150),
   (optional)

In a medium saucepan mix the salsa with the tomato purée, water, cumin and oregano, and bring to a boil. Reduce the heat and simmer for 15 minutes stirring occasionally.

Sauté the mince in 1 tablespoon of oil until lightly browned. Keep to one side. Then in a large frying pan lightly fry the tortillas in oil on one side for a few seconds only. Spread 4–6 tablespoons of the sauce over the bottom of a large ovenproof dish. Brush each tortilla with more of the sauce, then fill it with some of the cheese and mince, and ½ tablespoon of the chopped onions, and roll it into a tube. Place the tortilla seam-side down in the dish. Repeat with the other tortillas, reserving a little cheese and onion to garnish.

Spoon any remaining red sauce over the tortillas, and sprinkle them with the reserved cheese and onions and the olives. Bake at 180°F/350°F/gas 4 for 10–15 minutes. Serve at once, with the shredded lettuce and salsa verde if using.

Mung Bean Stew **v** *Kenya*

This is half-way between a soup and a stew, and is great served with plain boiled rice.

Preparation time:
1 hour
(plus soaking time)

SERVES 4

225g/8oz mung beans, soaked for a
   minimum of 8 hours
25g/1oz butter, margarine or ghee
2 cloves garlic, crushed
1 medium red onion, chopped
2 tbsp tomato purée

½ each green and red pepper, de-seeded
   and cut into small cubes
1 green chilli, de-seeded and chopped
   finely
300ml/½ pint water

Drain the mung beans and put them into a large saucepan. Cover the beans with water, and boil for 30–40 minutes until tender. Remove them from the heat: mash half with a fork or potato masher and leave the other half whole.

Heat the butter, margarine or ghee in a medium saucepan, add the garlic and onion and fry until golden brown. Add the tomato purée, the mashed beans, whole beans, then the peppers and chilli. Add the water, and mix well. Cover and simmer for about 20 minutes. Serve hot.

Red Enchiladas

Creole Vegetable Jambalaya v *USA*

Creole cooking followed the path of African peoples to America, where it developed its own character of well-seasoned ingredients and spicy sauces. Jambalaya is probably the most famous Creole dish, and cooked this way it is a pleasure to the eye as well as the palate.

Preparation time:
1 hour

SERVES 4–6

3 tbsp vegetable oil
1 small onion, chopped
1–2 cloves garlic, chopped
175g/6oz vegetarian mince
2 vegetarian sausages, defrosted and
  sliced into rounds
1 medium leek, sliced thinly
1/2 red pepper, de-seeded and sliced
1 stick celery, sliced
85g/3oz okra, trimmed, or courgette,
  diced
1 tsp dried thyme

1 tbsp freshly chopped basil
2 tsp Cajun Spice Mix (page 152)
175g/6oz long-grain rice
400g/14oz tinned chopped tomatoes
600ml/1 pint vegetable stock (page
  32), or water
225g/8oz small brown mushrooms,
  halved
sea salt and black pepper to taste
Tabasco to taste
chopped spring onions to garnish

In a large saucepan, heat the oil, and soften the onion and garlic over a medium heat for 5 minutes. Add the mince and sausages, and fry until browned. Then add the leek, red pepper, celery and okra or courgette, and stir until the vegetables have softened slightly. Add the herbs and Cajun Spice Mix, and stir well. Then stir in the rice until it is thoroughly incorporated.

Add the tomatoes and half the stock, and cook over a low heat, covered, for 10–15 minutes. Stir in the mushrooms and remaining stock and cook for a further 5–10 minutes until the rice is tender.

Season to taste with salt, pepper and Tabasco. Serve sprinkled with chopped spring onions.

RICE

Rice is a staple of the vegetarian diet. It comes in many different varieties, each of which has a different quality, flavour and aroma. Long grain is the most widely used type of white rice. It is best suited to dishes where the grains need to remain separate such as salads and pilafs. Risotto rice, such as Arborio, is a plump, short grain which, as its name suggests, is excellent for risottos and other Italian rice dishes. It works well as it is very starchy and remains moist and sticky. Basmati rice is available both brown and white. Its delicate aroma makes it ideal for Indian or Thai dishes. Brown rice has a nutty flavour and chewy texture. Wild rice is technically not rice at all, but an aquatic grass grown in America. As it is rather more expensive that the other varieties, it is often combined with long grain to add a little colour and contrast in flavour.

Tacos v *Mexico*

Crisp taco shells, filled and topped with shredded lettuce, cheese (omit for vegans) and salsa, make a nutritious and quick meal. You can experiment endlessly with fillings. Here are two of my favourites.

REFRIED BEAN FILLING

I always make my own refried beans but you could just as easily buy them in tins.

SUFFICIENT FOR 8–12 TACOS

225g/8oz pinto beans, soaked for a
  minimum of 8 hours
2 medium onions, 1 quartered and 1
  chopped

4 tbsp olive oil
½–1 tsp chilli powder (optional)
sea salt and black pepper to taste

In a large saucepan, cook the pinto beans with the quartered onion, generously covered with water until tender, for at least 1 hour. Drain, return them to the pan and mash them.

In a small frying pan fry the chopped onion in the oil with chilli powder (if using) until softened then add to the beans. Reheat the beans, stirring, and season to taste with salt.

MINCE FILLING

SUFFICIENT FOR 8–12 TACOS

1 medium onion, chopped finely
2 tbsp olive oil
225g/8oz vegetarian mince
1 small chilli, de-seeded and chopped,
  to taste
1 tsp ground cumin

½ tsp dried oregano
200g/7oz tinned chopped tomatoes,
  drained
400g/14oz tinned kidney beans
sea salt and black pepper to taste

In a medium saucepan, soften the onion in the oil over a medium heat for 5 minutes. Add the mince, chilli, cumin and oregano and simmer gently for 5 minutes, then add the tomatoes and beans, and simmer gently for another 5 minutes stirring occasionally. Season to taste.

Allow 2–3 taco shells per person. Spoon in a generous dollop of your chosen filling and top with shredded lettuce, grated cheese and/or sour cream or soya yoghurt, and Salsa (page 151).

Deep Dish Pie v *UK*

Savoury pie served with a mound of fluffy mashed potato is a British institution.

Preparation time:
45 minutes

Cooking time:
40 minutes

SERVES 6

2 medium onions, chopped
1 clove garlic, chopped
2 tbsp vegetable oil
225g/8oz flat mushrooms, chopped
450g/1lb vegetarian chunks or
    burgers, cubed
1 tsp fresh thyme
900ml/1½ pints Special Gravy (page
    149), or made from granules

2 tbsp soy sauce, or ½ tsp yeast extract
1 tbsp balsamic vinegar
sea salt and black pepper to taste
350g/12oz puff pastry
beaten free-range egg or soya milk
    to glaze

In a large saucepan fry the onions and garlic in the oil over a medium heat for about 4 minutes. Add the mushrooms and toss well.

Add the chunks or cubed burgers, and the thyme. Cook for 5 minutes over a low heat. Add the gravy and simmer gently for 15–20 minutes until it has thickened. Add the soy sauce or yeast extract and balsamic vinegar, and season with salt and pepper. Set aside to cool.

Place a china pastry support in the centre of a large pie dish, then spoon in the filling.

Roll out the pastry 5mm/¼ inch thick to the shape of the dish. Cut a strip 2cm/ ¾ inch wide from around the edge of the pastry. Continue rolling the main piece of pastry until it fits the dish once more. Dampen the rim of the dish with water, and place the pastry strip around it. Moisten the attached pastry strip, then cover with the pastry lid. Press the edges together firmly and trim the excess pastry. Use the back of a knife to make a decorative edge. You can re-roll the trimmings to make decorative leaves (see photograph opposite). Make a small round hole in the centre of the pie. Brush the pastry lid with beaten egg or milk.

Bake the pie in the oven at 230°C/450°F/gas 8 until the pastry has risen and turned lightly golden, about 10–12 minutes. Reduce the heat to 200°C/400°F/gas 6 and cook for a further 20–25 minutes until crisp and golden brown. Serve at once with Special Gravy and Special Mashed Potato (page 129).

Deep Dish Pie with
Special Mashed Potato
and Special Gravy

Pad Thai Noodles v *Thailand*

This dish combines all the tastes that the Thais cherish in their cuisine – sweet, sour and hot.

Preparation time:
30 minutes

SERVES 4

140g/5oz rice ribbon noodles
groundnut oil for frying
140g/5oz firm tofu, cut into rods
4 cloves garlic, chopped finely
1 large free-range egg, beaten (optional)
4 tbsp vegetable stock (page 32)
2 tbsp fresh lime juice
1 tbsp unrefined sugar
2 tbsp soy sauce

1 tsp sea salt
½ tsp dried chilli flakes
115g/4oz peanuts, chopped
450g/1lb beansprouts
3 spring onions, the whites cut thinly crosswise, the greens sliced into thin lengths
2 limes or 1 lemon, quartered lengthwise to garnish

In a medium bowl, soak the rice noodles in warm water according to packet instructions. Meanwhile, prepare all the other ingredients so that they are to hand once you start stir-frying. Heat about 2.5-cm/1-inch of the oil in a large wok and fry the tofu over a medium heat, turning the pieces until they are golden all over. Remove them with a slotted spoon and drain on kitchen paper.

Omit the following stage if not using the egg and go straight to*. Pour all but approximately 1 tablespoon of oil from the wok and heat until sizzling. Add the beaten egg and lightly scramble. Remove from the wok and put to one side. *Heat a further 2 tablespoons of oil, sauté the garlic, add the drained noodles and toss until they are coated with oil. Add the stock, lime juice, sugar and soy sauce, and toss well, gently pushing the noodles around the pan. Then add the tofu, egg, salt, chilli flakes and half of the peanuts, and turn the noodles again.

Finally, add all but a handful of the beansprouts and the spring onions. Turn for a further minute or two, until the beansprouts have softened slightly.

Arrange the noodles on a warm serving plate and garnish with the remaining peanuts and beansprouts. Place the lime and/or lemon wedges around the edge.

NOODLES

Noodles are becoming increasingly popular and offer an interesting alternative to rice or pasta. There are many different types – wheat, potato or rice flour and those made from soya or mung bean starch. Dried noodles are now available in most shops and the fresh ones can be found in specialist Chinese or Japanese shops. Egg noodles are made from wheat flour and egg and sold in flat sheets which separate when cooked. They are, of course, unsuitable for a vegan diet. Cellophane or glass noodles are made from ground mung bean flour and, although beautiful to look at, have a gelatinous texture which takes a little getting used to! Rice noodles – also known as rice vermicelli – are long, thin white strands. Ribbon noodles are made from ground rice and water. These are broad noodles which need to be soaked before cooking. As a general rule you should allow 90–125g/ 3–4oz of dried noodles per person.

Golden Pumpkin Curry v *India*

Preparation time:
30–35 minute

Pumpkin is one of my favourites. This warming, nourishing way of serving it is great with a bowl of basmati rice and warm naan bread.

SERVES 4

2 tbsp vegetable oil or ghee
$\frac{1}{2}$ tsp mustard seeds
2 large onions, sliced
4 cloves garlic, crushed
1-cm/$\frac{1}{2}$-inch piece of fresh ginger, peeled and grated
2 green chillies, deseeded and chopped
1 tsp turmeric powder

450g/1lb pumpkin, peeled, de-seeded and cubed
sea salt to taste
1 tsp unrefined sugar
150ml/$\frac{1}{4}$ pint vegetable stock (page 32), or water
freshly chopped coriander (or flat-leaf parsley if preferred) to garnish

In a medium saucepan, heat the oil or ghee and fry the mustard seeds over a medium heat for 1 minute. Then add the onions, garlic, ginger and chillies. Stir-fry for 5 minutes.

Add the turmeric and mix well, then add the pumpkin, a little salt and the sugar, and mix thoroughly. Cook gently, covered, for 10 minutes, stirring occasionally.

Then add the stock or water and continue to cook until the pumpkin is tender, for about another 5–10 minutes. Serve sprinkled with coriander or parsley.

Risotto Milanese ~ *Italy*

Preparation time:
35 minutes

Risotto Milanese is a classic dish – its simplicity is its charm. Serve it with the best Italian bread you can find and a simple tomato and red onion salad.

SERVES 4

1 medium red onion, chopped
85g/3oz butter or margarine
1 tbsp olive oil
280g/10oz risotto or arborio rice
1.2 litres/2 pints vegetable stock, warmed (page 32)

pinch of saffron strands
125ml/4fl oz dry white wine
50g/2oz vegetarian Parmesan, grated
sea salt and black pepper to taste

In a large saucepan, soften the onion in half the butter or margarine and all the oil over a medium heat, for about 5 minutes. Add the rice, and stir until it is thoroughly incorporated with the onion. Add the saffron and the wine. Add the warmed vegetable stock a ladle at a time, stirring constantly, adding more stock as the rice cooks and absorbs most of the liquid.

After 20 minutes, taste the rice. It should be just tender in the centre of the grain. Cook for a further 5 minutes if necessary. Stir in the Parmesan and remaining butter or margarine. Season to taste with salt and pepper.

Fontina and Tomato Pie ~ *Italy*

This beautiful looking dish from Piedmont in northern Italy is perfect for special occasions. If you can't find Fontina, use vegetarian Cheddar or a similar waxy cheese.

Preparation time:
30 minutes

Cooking time:
20–30 minutes

SERVES 6

15–20 slices focaccia or crusty white
  bread, cut about 1cm/½ inch thick
150ml/¼ pint dairy or soya milk
2 tbsp olive oil
1 medium red onion, sliced thinly
1 small yellow pepper, de-seeded and
  chopped

sea salt and black pepper to taste
225g/8oz Fontina cheese, grated
225g/8oz tomatoes, sliced thinly
4 large free-range eggs
50g/2oz grated vegetarian Parmesan
1 tbsp freshly chopped oregano

Dip the bread slices into the milk to soften, then line a buttered 23-cm/9-inch oven-proof dish with them, making a scalloped edge with the crusts. Bake for 15–20 minutes at 200°C/400°F/gas 6 until lightly golden.

In a medium frying pan, sauté the onion and yellow pepper in the oil until soft. Season with salt and pepper, and spoon it over the bread. Sprinkle with grated cheese and cover with the tomatoes.

Beat the eggs with the Parmesan and oregano and pour them over the pie filling. Return to the oven and bake for a further 20–30 minutes until the eggs have set.

Boston Slow-Baked Beans **V** *USA*

SERVES 4–6

Preparation time:
1 hour
(plus
soaking time)

Cooking time:
4 hours

450g/1lb dried haricot beans, soaked
  for a minimum of 8 hours
25g/1oz unrefined soft brown sugar
4–6 tbsp black treacle
1 tbsp dry mustard
1 medium onion, chopped
1 clove garlic

4 tbsp vegetarian Worcestershire sauce
4 tbsp tomato purée
450ml/¾ pint vegetable stock (page
  32)
450ml/¾ pint tomato juice
sea salt and black pepper to taste

Drain the beans, place them in a large flameproof casserole with sufficient water to cover. Bring to the boil and boil rapidly for 10 minutes, then simmer covered for 45 minutes.

Drain the beans and return them to the casserole with the remaining ingredients. Mix thoroughly, season with salt and pepper to taste, cover and bake in the oven at 150°C/300°F/gas 2 for 4 hours until the beans are tender.

Check and stir the beans occasionally during cooking and add a little water, if necessary, to prevent them from drying out. Taste and adjust the seasoning if necessary before serving.

Fontina and Tomato Pie

Goulash v *Hungary*

Hungary's most famous dish is comfort food at its best. There is nothing fashionable about it – it has stood the test of time because it is simply great food. I usually serve it with rice or Dumplings (page 152).

Preparation time:
1 hour

SERVES 6

2 tbsp olive oil
1 large onion, chopped
2 medium carrots, peeled and sliced
1 medium parsnip, peeled and cubed
350g/12oz vegetarian chunks or
    burgers, cubed
1–2 tbsp paprika to taste
400g/14oz tinned tomatoes
3 tbsp tomato purée

1 tsp caraway seeds
600ml/1 pint vegetable stock
2 medium potatoes, diced
sea salt and black pepper to taste
200ml/7fl oz crème fraîche, or warmed
    soya cream
paprika and finely chopped parsley to
    garnish

In a large saucepan, heat the olive oil and fry the onion, carrots and parsnip over a medium heat until they begin to brown, about 8 minutes.

Add the vegetarian chunks, paprika, tomatoes, tomato purée and caraway seeds. Heat gently and stir for 3–5 minutes.

Add the stock and the potatoes, and mix well. Bring to a simmer, cover and cook for a further 25–30 minutes until the potatoes are tender, adding more stock or water if needed.

Season to taste. Stir in the crème fraîche or soya cream, heat through gently, and garnish with a dusting of paprika and a sprinkling of parsley.

TIP
Use Hungarian paprika if you can find it. Some types of commercial paprika are only colouring agents and won't give you the desired authentic flavours.

Quesadillas ~ *Mexico*

Preparation time:
20 minutes

Cooking time:
5 minutes

Folded tortillas which contain various fillings are classic Mexican food. You can experiment using any kind of filling you choose.

MAKES 6

1 tbsp vegetable oil
1 small onion, chopped
225g/8oz vegetarian mince
4 tbsp freshly chopped coriander (or flat-leaf parsley if preferred)
2–3 tbsp vegetable stock (page 32)
6 large tortillas
300g/10½oz vegetarian Cheddar, grated

12 thin slices of tomato
12 thin slices of red onion
6 tbsp Salsa (page 151)
½ iceberg lettuce, shredded
1 large ripe avocado, diced
1 tbsp lemon juice
6 tbsp soured cream or soya yoghurt
4 spring onions, chopped finely

Heat the oil in a medium frying pan and sauté the onion and mince until lightly browned. Add half the coriander or parsley and the stock and cook for 2–3 minutes. Cover half of each tortilla with grated cheese, two slices of tomato and onion, and some mince. Fold the tortillas over, transfer to a baking tray, top with a little salsa, and bake at 200°C/400°F/gas 6 for about 5 minutes, until the cheese melts.

Meanwhile, mix the shredded lettuce with the avocado and lemon juice.

Spoon some soured cream or yoghurt over the top of each tortilla, sprinkle with chopped spring onions and the remaining coriander or parsley and serve at once, with the avocado mixture on the side.

Sauerkraut and Sausages **v** *Germany*

Preparation time:
1 hour 55 minutes

SERVES 6–8

2 large onions, sliced
2 tbsp vegetable oil
900g/2lb sauerkraut (pickled cabbage)
4 large carrots, sliced
12 juniper berries, crushed

300ml/½ pint vegetable stock (page 32)
16 vegetarian sausages, grilled until well browned

In a large flameproof casserole, soften the onions in the oil gently over a low to medium heat for about 10 minutes. Add the sauerkraut and the carrots, toss together well, then add the juniper berries.

Stir in the stock and simmer covered for 1½ hours. Add a little water if necessary to keep the mixture moist during cooking.

Add the sausages just before serving, mix them in well, and serve with a big bowl of Special Mashed Potato (page 129).

Vegetable Kichdi v *India*

Preparation time:
40 minutes

This wonderful Indian dish is aromatic and beautifully spiced. Serve with the Yoghurt with Fresh Mint (page 147), and warm naan bread.

SERVES 4–6

225g/8oz basmati rice
50g/2oz red lentils
25g/1oz butter, margarine or ghee
2 red chillies, de-seeded and chopped
1 tbsp cumin seeds
5 peppercorns, crushed
4 green cardamom pods
4 cloves
2.5-cm/1-inch stick cinnamon
1 tsp turmeric powder, or 1 or 2
   strands of saffron

2 large onions, chopped finely
5-cm/2-inch piece fresh ginger, grated
1 large potato, peeled and diced
1 large tomato, skinned and chopped
50g/2oz frozen peas
50g/2oz each cauliflower and broccoli
   florets
600ml/1 pint water
sea salt
cashew nuts, toasted (page 70), to
   garnish

Rinse the rice with the lentils in a large sieve.

In a large frying pan, heat the butter, margarine or ghee and fry the spices over a medium heat. When they sizzle and crackle, add the chopped onions and ginger and fry until golden brown.

Next, add the prepared vegetables, rice, lentils and salt and stir in the water. Stir and simmer for approximately 15–20 minutes until the rice is cooked, adding more water if necessary. Stir and serve sprinkled with the cashew nuts.

Grilled Spicy Tofu v *Senegal*

Preparation time:
15–20 minutes,
(plus
marinating time)

A very unusual dish from Senegal with tempting flavours and textures.

SERVES 4–6

115g/4oz crunchy (wholenut)
   peanut butter
3 tbsp groundnut oil
50ml/2fl oz lemon juice
2 large onions, chopped
2 chillies, chopped
2 cloves garlic, chopped

2 sprigs thyme, chopped finely
1 bay leaf, crumbled
sea salt and black pepper to taste
2 large tinned pimentos, cut into strips
450g/1lb firm tofu, cut into 1-cm/
   ½-inch cubes

In a large flameproof dish, combine the peanut butter, groundnut oil, half of the lemon juice, the onions, chillies, garlic, thyme, bay leaf and the pimentos. Season with salt and pepper. Place the tofu in this marinade and leave for at least 30 minutes.

Pre-heat the grill to high for 5 minutes.

Place the dish of marinated tofu under the grill until it has browned on top. Turn and brown again, then twice more until the tofu is golden brown all over. Serve with rice.

Banana and Yam Stew v *Tanzania*

SERVES 6

150ml/¼ pint groundnut oil
900g/2lb yam, peeled and cubed
1 green chilli, de-seeded and chopped
1 tbsp freshly chopped coriander
1 medium red onion, chopped
1 large tomato, skinned and quartered
1 large carrot, diced
2 cloves garlic, chopped
1 tsp each ground cloves,
   turmeric and cumin

sea salt and black pepper to taste
300ml/½ pint coconut milk
1.2 litres/2 pints vegetable stock
   (page 32)
2 bay leaves
1 tbsp cornflour, mixed with 2 tbsp
   cold water
2 green bananas, peeled and sliced
   thickly

In a large saucepan, heat the oil and sauté the yam pieces over a medium heat until they are golden brown. Remove them from the pan with a slotted spoon.

Reduce the heat and in the same oil sauté the chilli, coriander, onion, tomato, carrot, garlic and cloves with the spices. Season with salt and pepper.

Add the coconut milk and the stock, and bring to the boil. Add the bay leaves, then lower the heat to a simmer. Stir in the cornflour mixture.

Add the yams and bananas and season to taste with salt and pepper. Cover and simmer gently for 30 minutes. Check the seasoning, then allow the stew to rest for 10 minutes and remove the bay leaves before serving it with rice.

*Preparation time:
1¼ hours*

COCONUT MILK

Coconut milk can be bought ready to use or made from creamed, fresh or desiccated coconut. The liquid inside a coconut is a thin, sweet and rather watery fluid and should not be confused with coconut milk as a cooking ingredient.

Green Curry v *Thailand*

If you are in a hurry, you can buy ready-made Thai green curry paste, but it is worth making your own if you can. Serve with rice.

SERVES 2–3

2 tbsp vegetable or groundnut oil
1–2 tbsp Green Curry Paste (page 149)
300ml/½ pint coconut milk
1 small aubergine, cubed
225g/8oz tinned bamboo shoots,
   drained

1 medium onion, diced
1 tbsp unrefined caster sugar
1 tsp soy sauce
1 medium courgette, cubed
chopped coriander (or flat-leaf parsley
   if preferred), to garnish

In a medium saucepan, heat the oil over a medium heat and stir in the curry paste for a few seconds. Gradually add the coconut milk and heat it through, mixing well, for 3 minutes. Add the aubergine, bamboo shoots and chopped onion, and stir gently for 5 minutes. Stir in the sugar and soy sauce, and mix well.

Bring the mixture to the boil, then simmer gently for 10 minutes, adding a little water to moisten it if necessary. Add the courgette and cook for a further 5 minutes. Remove the pan from the heat and leave it to stand for a few minutes.

Transfer the curry into a bowl and sprinkle with chopped coriander or parsley.

*Preparation time:
35–40 minutes*

Bean and Sweet Potato Nachos ~ *Mexico*

Preparation time:
1¼ hours

These substantial nachos are not as complicated as they may look at first glance and are well worth a try.

SERVES 4

700g/1lb 9oz sweet potato, peeled and
  diced
3 tbsp olive oil
2 tsp cumin seeds
2 tsp coriander seeds
1 medium onion, sliced thinly
2 cloves garlic, crushed
1 small red chilli, de-seeded and
  chopped finely
1 tsp paprika
400g/14oz tinned chopped tomatoes
½ each medium red and green pepper,
  de-seeded and diced

280g/10oz tinned red kidney beans,
  rinsed and drained
225g/8oz tortilla (corn) chips
225g/8oz vegetarian Cheddar, grated
2 tbsp freshly chopped coriander (or
  flat-leaf parsley if preferred)
1 medium avocado, peeled, stoned and
  sliced
125ml/4fl oz soured cream or plain
  soya yoghurt

In a large baking dish, mix the sweet potato, 2 tablespoons of the oil and the spices and bake, uncovered, at 180°C/350°F/gas 4 for 50–60 minutes, until tender.

Heat the remaining oil gently in a pan and add the onion, garlic, chilli and paprika. Cover and cook until the onion is soft, about 10 minutes, stirring occasionally. Add the tomatoes with their juices and the peppers, and simmer uncovered for 5 minutes. Stir in the beans.

Divide the corn chips among four individual ovenproof dishes and top with the bean mixture, then with the sweet potato and finish with the cheese. Bake for 10 minutes until the nachos are well heated through and the cheese has melted.

Serve sprinkled with coriander or parsley, with avocado and soured cream or yoghurt served separately.

Minted Couscous with Roasted Vegetables

v *Morocco*

Couscous, traditional Berber food, is one of North Africa's great dishes. Here, mixed with lemon juice and mint and served with roasted vegetables, it makes a memorable meal.

ROASTED VEGETABLES

Preparation time:
20 minutes
(plus 3–4 hours
marinating time)

Cooking time:
30–35 minutes

SERVES 4

1 large aubergine, cut into chunky
  batons
450g/1lb courgettes, cut into chunky
  batons
1 large red onion, cut into 8 wedges
12 cloves garlic, in their skins
10 basil leaves, torn roughly

1 sprig freshly chopped rosemary
4–6 tbsp olive oil
1 each red and yellow pepper, grilled,
  skinned, quartered and de-seeded
4 field mushrooms, sliced
15–20 black olives, pitted

Put the prepared aubergine, courgettes, onion and garlic into a large bowl with the basil and rosemary. Sprinkle with half the olive oil and toss well. Leave to stand at room temperature for 3–4 hours.

Pre-heat the oven to 220°C/425°F/gas 7. Spread the vegetables on to a baking tray or trays, in a single layer, and drizzle with the remaining olive oil. Roast for 15 minutes, then add the peppers, mushrooms and olives, and toss. Return to the oven and roast for a further 10–15 minutes until the vegetables are tender, turning once more before the end of the cooking time.

MINTED COUSCOUS

Preparation time:
20 minutes

SERVES 4

225g/8oz couscous
600ml/1 pint water, boiled
150ml/¼ pint olive oil
zest and juice of 2 lemons
1 yellow pepper, de-seeded and
  chopped finely

4 spring onions, chopped finely
4–6 tbsp freshly chopped mint
sea salt and black pepper to taste

Put the couscous into a large bowl and pour the boiling water over it. Stir for a couple of minutes and leave it until the water has absorbed and the couscous is tender, about 6–7 minutes.

Add the olive oil, lemon juice and zest, and mix them in thoroughly.

Stir in the chopped pepper, spring onions and mint. Season with salt and pepper, and serve with the roasted vegetables.

Minted Couscous with
Roasted Vegetables

Spanokopitta ~ *Greece*

This classic Greek dish combines crisp filo pastry with spinach, leeks and dill. Serve with the Cephalonian Salad (page 55).

Preparation time:
40 minutes

Cooking time:
45–50 minutes

SERVES 6–8

450g/1lb leeks, washed and sliced
   thinly
6 tbsp olive oil
900g/2lb fresh spinach, washed and
   trimmed, or 450g/1lb frozen spinach
225g/8oz vegetarian feta cheese
3 large free-range eggs, beaten
150ml/¼ pint dairy or soya milk

1 tbsp freshly chopped dill or fennel
½ tsp ground nutmeg
sea salt and black pepper to taste
8 spring onions, sliced
115g/4oz pine nuts (page 70), toasted
225g/8oz filo pastry

In a large frying pan, sauté the leeks in 2 tablespoons of olive oil until they soften. In a large saucepan wilt the spinach over a high heat and drain it thoroughly in a colander. Squeeze out excess water.

In a large bowl, mash the feta with a fork and add the beaten eggs, milk, dill or fennel and nutmeg, and season well with salt and pepper. Add the prepared spinach, leeks, spring onions and pine nuts, and fold these into the mixture.

Grease a 23-cm/9-inch square baking tin and line with half of the pastry sheets. To do this, lay them down one at a time, brushing each one with olive oil. Next, spread the filling evenly over the pastry base. To finish, layer the remaining pastry sheets over the top, again brushing each one liberally with the olive oil, especially the last sheet.

Bake at 190°C/375°F/gas 5 for 40–45 minutes, until the top of the pie is golden and crisp. Allow it to cool a little before cutting it into squares with a sharp knife.

Traditional Artichoke Pie ~ *Italy*

Preparation time:
25 minutes

Cooking time:
40–45 minutes

This is a classic Italian party dish *par excellence* – as beautiful to look at as it is to eat. Serve it either hot or warm, with a choice of salads.

SERVES 6–8

25g/1oz butter or margarine
125–175ml/4–6fl oz olive oil
2 x 400g/14oz tins artichoke hearts, drained and cut in half
350g/12oz mushrooms, sliced
2 tbsp freshly chopped parsley
1 clove garlic, crushed
225g/8oz ricotta cheese

3 large free-range eggs
4 tbsp vegetarian Parmesan cheese, grated
½ tsp ground nutmeg
sea salt and black pepper to taste
225g/8oz filo pastry
50g/2oz hazelnuts, toasted (page 70) and chopped

In a large frying pan, heat the butter or margarine with 2 tablespoons of oil and cook the artichokes, mushrooms, parsley and garlic gently for 5 minutes over a medium heat. Set aside.

Mix the ricotta with the eggs and Parmesan in a large bowl. Season to taste with nutmeg, salt and pepper.

Grease a 23-cm/9-inch square baking tin and line with half of the pastry sheets. To do this, lay them down one at a time, brushing each one with olive oil.

Spread the artichoke heart and mushroom mixture over the pastry, followed by the ricotta mixture. Scatter the toasted hazelnuts over the top.

To finish, layer the remaining pastry sheets over the top, again brushing each one liberally with the olive oil, especially the last. Bake at 180°C/350°F/gas 4 for 40–45 minutes until the top has puffed up and turned golden.

Overleaf: Greek Menu (see Menu Planner on page 184)

Black-eyed Bean Stew with Spicy Pumpkin

v *Africa*

This dish is, in fact, two stews served together. Invest a little time and effort, and your reward will be a hearty, intensely flavoured meal.

Preparation time:
30 minutes

SERVES 4

BEAN STEW

4 tbsp groundnut oil
1 large onion, chopped
2 large carrots, sliced
1 green or red pepper, de-seeded and chopped
2 cloves garlic, chopped
1 tbsp freshly chopped, or 1 tsp dried, thyme
1 tsp paprika
½ tsp mixed spice
300ml/½ pint vegetable stock (page 32)
2 x 400g/14oz tins black-eyed beans
sea salt and black pepper to taste
Tabasco to taste

SPICY PUMPKIN

25g/1oz butter or margarine
700g/1lb 9oz pumpkin, cubed
1 medium onion, chopped finely
2 cloves garlic, crushed
3 tomatoes, skinned and chopped
1 tsp ground cinnamon
2 tsp curry powder
pinch of grated nutmeg
300ml/½ pint water
sea salt and black pepper to taste

To make the bean stew: in a large saucepan, sauté the onion, carrots, pepper, garlic, thyme and spices in the oil, for about 5 minutes. Add the stock, bring to the boil, reduce the heat to a simmer, stir in the beans and season to taste with salt, pepper and Tabasco. Cover and simmer for 15 minutes, adding more stock or water as necessary until the vegetables are tender.

To make the spicy pumpkin: melt the butter or margarine in a large saucepan over a medium heat. Add the pumpkin, onion, garlic, tomatoes, spices and water. Stir well and simmer, covered until the pumpkin is tender, about 10–15 minutes. Season to taste with salt and pepper. Serve with the black-eyed beans and a dish of rice or couscous.

PUMPKIN

Pumpkins are native to America but have been known in Britain since the sixteenth century. I grow them very successfully in my own garden! They can grow to enormous size and many pumpkins are larger than the average household might want, so it is well worth having more than one recipe up your sleeve before you buy one. As well as the traditional pumpkin pie, I use my own crop to make delicious soups, risottos or I oven roast chunks along with other winter vegetables. It is useful to remember that pumpkin contains a lot of water and will cook down to approximately half its bulk.

Black-eyed Bean Stew with
Spicy Pumpkin

Party Nut Loaf ~ *UK*

This fabulous loaf looks wonderful and slices very well, even when hot. It is a great party dish served with the Roasted Red Pepper Sauce (page 149).

Preparation time:
45 minutes

Cooking time:
40 minutes

SERVES 8

115g/4oz butter or margarine
1 large onion, chopped finely
1½ tbsp plain flour
4–5 tbsp dairy or soya milk
3 large free-range eggs, separated
200g/7oz unsalted cashew nuts, ground finely
175g/6oz brazil nuts, ground finely
200g/7oz brown breadcrumbs
50g/2oz mature vegetarian Cheddar, grated
1 tbsp freshly chopped parsley

FILLING

4 shallots, chopped
85g/3oz mushrooms, chopped
1 medium courgette, grated
1 tsp each freshly chopped thyme, rosemary and sage
2 tbsp each freshly chopped parsley and chives
¼ tsp ground nutmeg
sea salt and black pepper to taste

Butter a 900g/2lb loaf tin and line it with well-greased non-stick baking parchment.

In a medium saucepan, melt 25g/1oz of the butter or margarine and soften the onion over a medium heat for about 5 minutes. Stir in the flour and cook for a further minute. Gradually add the milk, stirring continuously until the mixture thickens. Simmer for 2 minutes, then remove the pan from the heat. Cool then beat in the egg whites (put the yolks to one side for the filling), nuts, breadcrumbs, cheese and parsley, and mix well. Put aside until you have prepared the filling.

To make the filling, cook the shallots in the remaining butter or margarine in a medium pan until soft, then add the mushrooms and cook over a high heat until browned. Add the courgette to the pan and cook over a medium heat for 2–3 minutes until the juices run, then add the herbs and nutmeg. Season to taste with salt and pepper and remove from the heat. Allow to cool slightly, then stir in the egg yolks.

Spread half of the nut mixture into the prepared loaf tin and spoon the mushroom and courgette filling on top and cover with the remaining nut mixture.

Bake at 180°C/350°F/gas 4 for 40 minutes or until firm. Leave to stand for 10 minutes before turning out the loaf on to a serving plate and slice it using a very sharp knife.

Festive Loaf ~ *USA*

Preparation time:
15 minutes

Cooking time:
40–45 minutes

The simplicity of this loaf is as much its appeal as the delicious flavours and textures. Served with all the trimmings, it is a fitting centrepiece for any festive occasion.

SERVES 8

4 tbsp olive oil
2 medium onions, chopped
16 vegetarian burgers, defrosted and crumbled
2 tbsp each freshly chopped sage and rosemary

4 large free-range eggs, beaten
6 tbsp single soya cream
4 tbsp tamari or soy sauce

In a large frying pan, heat the olive oil and sauté the onion until soft. Add the crumbled burgers and brown them with the onion, taking care that they do not stick to the pan. Add the herbs and fry for a further 2 minutes before removing the pan from the heat.

Place in a bowl and add the beaten eggs, soya cream and tamari or soy sauce. Mix well. Press the mixture into a 900g/2lb well-greased loaf tin and bake at 180°C/350°F/gas 4 for 40–45 minutes until it has set in the centre.

Leave the loaf in the tin to cool, and turn it out carefully after 15 minutes. Serve warm, with Special Gravy (page 149) or Onion and Juniper Gravy (page 151), Cranberry Sauce (page 148), and Herby Stuffing (page 153).

Quiche Linda ~ *France*

Preparation time:
40 minutes

Cooking time:
30 minutes

My version of a French classic, this quiche rises beautifully and is exquisitely light and fluffy. Serve with the Fennel and Rocket Salad (page 50).

SERVES 6

225g/8oz shortcrust pastry (page 153)
1 large onion, chopped
6 slices vegetarian bacon, chopped
1 tbsp olive oil
4 large free-range eggs, beaten

175g/6oz vegetarian Cheddar, grated
sea salt and black pepper to taste
150ml/¼ pint dairy or soya milk or single dairy or soya cream

Roll out the pastry and line a 23-cm/9-inch flan case and bake blind (see page 161). Set aside to cool.

Meanwhile, in a medium frying pan, sauté the onion and bacon in the oil for 2–3 minutes, stirring until the onion is soft and the bacon is golden.

Whisk the eggs until foamy and fold in the onion, bacon and grated cheese. Season to taste with salt and pepper. Finally, add the milk or cream. Pour the mixture into the pastry case.

Bake at 200°C/400°F/gas 6 for 30 minutes, until it puffs up and rises well. Serve immediately.

Asparagus and Lemon Risotto **v** *Italy*

To get the best flavours from this dish, use fresh young asparagus.

Preparation time:
40 minutes

SERVES 4–6

3 tbsp olive oil
2 shallots, chopped
1 clove garlic, chopped finely
1 stick celery, chopped small
280g/10oz arborio or risotto rice
1 litre/1¾ pints vegetable stock
  (page 32), warmed
1 bunch asparagus, trimmed and
  chopped into 5-cm/2-inch pieces

6 fresh sage leaves, chopped finely
1 sprig rosemary, chopped finely
juice and grated zest of ½ lemon
50g/2oz goats' cheese or 4 tbsp soya
  cream
sea salt and black pepper to taste
flat-leaf parsley or grated Parmesan, to
  garnish

In a large saucepan, heat the oil and cook the shallots, garlic and celery over a medium heat for 4 minutes. Add the rice and stir well. Add 2 ladles of the warmed stock and stir until the rice has absorbed most of the liquid. Keep adding the stock gradually for about 10 more minutes, stirring constantly.

Add the asparagus, the herbs and lemon zest, and continue to cook gently, stirring for a further 10 minutes. At no point should you allow the mixture to become too dry – add more stock as necessary.

When the rice is cooked, mix in the goats' cheese or soya cream and lemon juice, season to taste with salt and pepper and sprinkle with the parsley or Parmesan just before serving.

TIP

You can add the tough ends of asparagus spears to your vegetable stock. This will give the risotto more flavour.

PRESERVING HERBS

It is possible to preserve fresh herbs by drying or freezing them. The herbs most suited to drying are marjoram, oregano, mint, rosemary and thyme. Just tie the stalks in bunches and hang them upside down in a warm airy place until dry or alternatively spread the sprigs out on racks or trays, cover with a fine cloth such as muslin, and leave in a warm, airy room for about 24 hours. Another option is freezing – herbs such as basil, chervil, dill, tarragon and parsley are the most successful. Simply pack the leaves or sprigs in small plastic freezer bags or add chopped herbs to water and freeze in ice-cube trays. Freezing actually retains the fresh flavour far better than drying so it is a good habit to adopt – especially as fresh herbs bought in shops can be quite costly.

Asparagus and Lemon Risotto

International Pizzas

The first pizzas were made in Naples in the early 1800s, but flat bread made from wheat-based yeast dough had been made there for centuries. Today it is enjoyed all over the world and different variations have been created to suit the local specialities.

A real Italian pizza is cooked in a wood-fired brick oven which is so hot that it is cooked in only a few minutes. However, with pizza stones and a hot oven, you can also achieve excellent results at home. Use a slab of unglazed terracotta from a tile centre and it will cost you a fraction of the price of the pizza stones you find in specialist kitchenware shops.

BASIC PIZZA DOUGH V

MAKES 4 X 23-CM/9-INCH PIZZA BASES OR
2 X 30-CM/12-INCH PIZZA BASES

300ml/½ pint water (¼
  boiling to ¼ cold)
2 tsp dried yeast
2 tbsp extra-virgin olive oil

1 tsp unrefined caster sugar
450g/1lb strong or plain
  white flour
pinch of sea salt

Mix the water, yeast, oil and sugar together in a small bowl and leave to stand for a few minutes. Sift the flour and salt into a large bowl and make a well in the centre. Stir in the yeast mixture to form a mass. Turn out on to a floured surface and knead it firmly for at least 10 minutes until it becomes elastic. Place it in a large, greased bowl and cover with a damp tea towel or plate. Leave it to rise for about 2 hours – until doubled in size.

Turn it out on to a floured surface and punch it down. Cut it into four pieces of equal size and roll these into balls (you can refrigerate or freeze the dough at this stage). Take one ball at a time and, using a rolling pin, roll it out until it is thin and about 23cm/9 inches in diameter. Arrange the topping of your choice on the base, lift carefully on to an oiled and pre-heated baking tray or pizza stone. Bake in a pre-heated oven at 230°C/450°F/gas 8 for 15–20 minutes until the outside edge is golden and the topping is cooked through.

Preparation time:
45 minutes
(plus 2 hours
proving)

Cooking time:
15–20 minutes

TIP
Try adding fresh herbs, sun-dried tomatoes, chopped chillies, etc. to the pizza base mixture before cooking.

English Breakfast Pizza ~ *UK*

FOR 1 X 30-CM/12-INCH PIZZA BASE (SEE BASIC RECIPE ON PAGE 116)

3 tbsp tomato purée
2–3 vegetarian sausages, lightly
  browned and cut in half crosswise
4 slices vegetarian bacon slices, sautéd
  lightly
2 tomatoes, sliced thickly

2 medium mushrooms, sliced
sea salt and black pepper to taste
olive oil, to drizzle
85g/3oz vegetarian mozzarella, sliced
1 poached free-range egg per person
  (optional)

Preparation time:
20 minutes

Cooking time:
15–20 minutes

Spread the tomato purée over the pizza base. Arrange the prepared sausages, bacon, tomatoes and mushrooms over the top. Season to taste, drizzle with a little olive oil and cover with the sliced mozzarella.

Bake at 230°C/450°F/gas 8 for 15–20 minutes until the base is crisp and the topping is lightly browned.

If you are using them, have the freshly poached eggs ready for the end of the cooking time, slip them on top and serve at once.

California Vegetable Pizza ~ *USA*

(See photograph on pages 116–7)

FOR 1 X 30-CM/12-INCH PIZZA BASE (SEE BASIC RECIPE ON PAGE 116)

3 tbsp Salsa (page 151)
8–10 spinach leaves, sautéd briefly in a
  little oil
6–8 baby corn
40g/1½oz mangetout, blanched briefly
  and sliced in half
½ yellow pepper, de-seeded, roasted,
  peeled and sliced

½ ripe avocado, sliced
50g/2oz cherry tomatoes, cut in half
sea salt and black pepper to taste
85g/3oz vegetarian mozzarella, sliced
1 tbsp olive oil
freshly chopped or dried marjoram or
  oregano

Preparation time:
15–20 minutes

Cooking time:
15–20 minutes

Spread the pizza base with the salsa. Arrange the prepared vegetables decoratively over the top and season to taste. Cover with the sliced mozzarella and brush the rim of the pizza with olive oil.

Bake at 230°C/450°F/gas 8 for 15–20 minutes until the base is crisp and the topping is lightly browned.

Siam Pizza ~ *Thailand*

Preparation time:
10–15 minutes

Cooking time:
15–20 minutes

FOR 1 X 30-CM/12-INCH PIZZA BASE (SEE BASIC RECIPE ON PAGE 116)

3 tbsp Satay Sauce (page 148)
50g/2oz carrots, coarsely grated
3–4 spring onions, chopped
50g/2oz marinated tofu (page 74)
soy sauce, to taste
1–2 tbsp olive oil

freshly chopped coriander (or flat-leaf
   parsley if preferred)
a little finely chopped chilli to taste
   (optional)
2 tsp sesame seeds
85g/3oz vegetarian mozzarella, sliced

Spread the pizza base with the satay sauce, then the carrots and sprinkle with the spring onions. Arrange the tofu over the top, drizzle with a little soy sauce to taste and a little of the olive oil. Sprinkle on the chopped coriander or parsley, then the optional chilli and sesame seeds. Cover with the sliced mozzarella. Brush the rim of the pizza with the rest of the oil.

Bake at 230°C/450°F/gas 8 for 15–20 minutes until the base is crisp and the topping lightly browned.

Athenian Pizza ~ *Greece*

Preparation time:
15 minutes

Cooking time:
15–20 minutes

FOR 1 X 30-CM/12-INCH PIZZA BASE (SEE BASIC RECIPE ON PAGE 116)

2 tbsp extra-virgin olive oil
1 small red onion, sliced
50g/2oz mushrooms, sliced
10 black olives, pitted
40g/1½oz peperoncini (pickled mild
   peppers), sliced

50g/2oz vegetarian feta
1 tbsp freshly chopped oregano or basil
sea salt and black pepper to taste
fresh oregano sprigs or basil leaves to
   garnish

Spread the pizza base with some of the olive oil. Arrange the onion, mushrooms, olives and peperoncini on the base. Crumble the feta over the top, and sprinkle with the oregano or basil. Season liberally and drizzle with the rest of the olive oil.

Bake at 230°C/450°F/gas 8 for 15–20 minutes until the base is crisp and the topping lightly browned. Garnish with a sprig or two of fresh oregano or basil leaves.

GREAT PIZZA TOPPINGS

* Roasted red onion with vegetarian Gorgonzola and rosemary (see photograph on page 117)
* Rocket, artichokes, olives, vegetarian mozzarella and Parmesan
* Roasted garlic, sun-dried tomatoes, herbs and vegetarian feta
* Roasted potato, garlic, cooked leeks, fresh thyme and vegetarian mozzarella
* Sliced roasted red pepper, sautéd with finely sliced leek and topped with vegetarian pecorino
* Caramelized Onions (page 131), capers, roasted aubergines with balsamic vinegar, Pesto Sauce (page 148), vegetarian mozzarella and Parmesan
* Aubergine cooked in Sichuan Sauce (page 18), chopped red onion and vegetarian mozzarella
* Fresh spinach leaves with garlic, pine nuts, raisins and vegetarian Fontina
* Pickled jalapeños, coriander, Salsa (page 151), pinto beans, mashed avocado or guacamole, soured cream and mature vegetarian Cheddar or Monteray Jack cheese
* Stir-fried Mangetout with Ginger and Garlic (page 126), tofu pieces and sweetcorn

BUILD YOUR OWN PIZZA PARTY

Have a pile of freshly baked pizza bases and invite your guests to show their originality by mixing their own ingredients for toppings. Lay out a buffet table with the ingredients below, and make a large tossed salad to go with the pizzas. A good rustic red wine and a couple of your favourite desserts will make a perfect feast.

* sliced fresh tomatoes
* sliced peppers, all colours
* thinly sliced red onion
* chopped spring onions
* coarsely chopped garlic cloves
* assorted pitted olives
* Pesto Sauce (page 148)
* sun-dried tomatoes
* rocket leaves
* pineapple rings
* capers
* quartered tinned artichoke hearts
* sautéd or grilled aubergine slices
* assorted vegetarian cheeses, grated and sliced, e.g. mozzarella, Cheddar, Fontina, Gouda or Gorgonzola

* tomato sauce or Salsa (page 151)
* grated vegetarian Parmesan
* bowls of olive oil, with brushes
* a big bowl of fresh chopped herbs
* sea salt and black pepper to taste

Preparation time:
30 minutes

Cooking time:
40 minutes

Tuscan Beans with Tomatoes, Garlic and Sage

v *Italy*

Preparation time:
30–40 minutes

This rich bean dish is dominated by the delicious flavour of sage and garlic. Serve with a crisp green salad.

SERVES 4

SKINNING TOMATOES

Put tomatoes into a large bowl and cover with boiling water. Leave to stand for about 30 seconds. Lift out one by one and pierce the skin with a sharp knife; the skin will peel off easily.

1 medium onion, chopped
3 cloves garlic, chopped
3 tbsp olive oil
300g/10½oz tinned haricot or
    cannellini beans, or butterbeans
300g/10½oz spinach, washed and dried

2 large ripe tomatoes, skinned and
    chopped (see tip)
2 tbsp freshly chopped sage
sea salt and black pepper to taste
300ml/½ pint vegetable stock (page 32)
4 rounds of ciabatta bread, toasted

In a large saucepan, sauté the onion and garlic in the oil over a medium heat until slightly softened, about 3–4 minutes. Add the drained beans, spinach, tomatoes and sage to the pan. Add 150ml/¼ pint of vegetable stock. Cover and simmer over a very low heat for about 15 minutes, topping up with stock as necessary. Season to taste with salt and pepper. Put a round of toasted bread into each serving bowl and ladle some of the beans over the top.

Artichoke Casserole with Pine Nuts v *Spain*

This rich, peasant-style casserole is particularly good served with a crusty loaf of bread to soak up the juices.

SERVES 4

Preparation time
50 minutes

3 tbsp olive oil
4 vegetarian bacon slices, cut into strips
1 large onion, chopped
3 cloves garlic, chopped
450g/1lb ripe plum tomatoes, skinned
    and chopped (see tip)

600ml/1 pint vegetable stock (page 32)
2 x 400g/14oz tins artichoke hearts,
    drained and halved
sea salt and black pepper to taste
25g/1oz pine nuts, toasted (page 70)

In a small frying pan, heat 1 tablespoon of the oil and cook the bacon over a medium heat until lightly browned. Remove from the pan and set to one side.

Heat the remaining oil in a large saucepan and soften the onion and garlic over a low heat for 5–7 minutes. Stir in the prepared tomatoes and cook uncovered for 10 minutes or until the tomatoes are reduced to a sauce consistency. Add the stock and season with salt and pepper. Bring to the boil, add the artichokes, cover and simmer for 12–15 minutes.

Turn the casserole out into a serving dish and sprinkle with the cooked bacon pieces and pine nuts. Serve immediately.

Aubergine, Sweet Potato and Goats' Cheese Gratin ~ *UK*

Preparation time:
40 minutes

Cooking time:
30 minutes

This was created by my friend Joanne. It is an unusual combination that really works. Everyone who has it thinks it is wonderful.

SERVES 6

2 medium aubergines, sliced diagonally
  1-cm/½-inch thick
4 tbsp olive oil
5 cloves garlic, sliced in half lengthwise
sea salt and black pepper to taste
2 tbsp balsamic vinegar
6 medium sweet potatoes, peeled and
  sliced 1-cm/½-inch thick

40g/1½oz vegetarian Parmesan, grated
75g/3oz vegetarian Cheddar, grated
handful of fresh basil leaves
225g/8oz vegetarian goats' cheese, sliced
1 quantity Roasted Red Pepper Sauce
  (page 149)

Lay the aubergine slices on a baking tray and brush them with olive oil. Turn them over and scatter with the garlic slices and brush with a little more oil. Season with salt and pepper and bake at 220°C/425°F/gas 7. Turn when lightly browned, after about 10 minutes, bake for another 10 minutes, then remove from the oven. Drizzle with balsamic vinegar and leave to cool.

In a large saucepan, blanch the sweet potato slices in boiling water for 3–4 minutes. Drain and cool.

Layer half of the sweet potatoes in a large baking dish. Sprinkle with one-third of the Parmesan and Cheddar and season with salt and pepper. Arrange half the basil leaves evenly on top. Lay half of the aubergine slices over the basil and distribute the halved garlic cloves evenly. Place half of the goats' cheese slices over the top. Repeat the layers and sprinkle with the remaining third of the Parmesan and Cheddar.

Bake at 200°C/400°F/gas 6 for 30 minutes until lightly browned on top.

Butternut Squash Pilaf v *Morocco*

This dish is typical of North Africa where sugar and sweet spices are often used in savoury recipes.

Preparation time
30 minutes

Cooking time
20-30 minutes

SERVES 4

1 large onion, chopped
125–150g/4–5oz butter or margarine
225g/8oz long grain rice
1 red chilli, de-seeded and chopped
3 whole cloves
2 tbsp sultanas
600ml/1 pint water

sea salt and black pepper to taste
1 butternut squash weighing about
   700g/1lb 9oz, peeled and cubed
50g/2oz unrefined demerara sugar
2 tsp ground cinnamon
1 tsp ground allspice

In a large saucepan, sauté the onion in 50g/2oz butter for about 5 minutes until softened. Add the rice, chilli, cloves and sultanas and stir thoroughly. Add the water and bring to the boil. Reduce the heat, cover and simmer for about 15 minutes until the water has been absorbed. Season to taste with salt and pepper.

Steam the squash for about 5 minutes until just tender. Butter a large overproof dish and sprinkle the base with 1 tablespoon of sugar. Mix the remaining sugar with the spices. Melt the remaining butter or margarine.

Arrange half the squash in the dish, sprinkle with half the spice mixture and drizzle with half the remaining butter or margarine. Spoon the rice on top then repeat the layer once more finishing with the butter or margarine.

Bake in the oven at 200°C/400°F/gas 6 for 20–30 minutes until lightly caramelised on the surface.

Serve at once with sautéd mushrooms, or grilled aubergine slices and some warmed pitta bread.

CHILLIES

Chillies come in many varieties. The plump red or green Jalapeño chilli is perhaps the best-known hot type and often used in Mexican cooking. Anaheims can also be red or green and are about 10cm/4 inches long with a blunt end but can be quite mild – a good choice for the timid. Thai or birdseye chillies are the tiniest of all but don't be fooled – they are extremely hot! They can be green, white, orange and red, and are sharply pointed and very pretty. Whichever chilli you choose always remove the seeds and veins first. I always keep a store of dried red chillies (often Poblanos) in the kitchen cupboard, but they can be very hot. Tinned chillies tend to be milder and are a truly delicious way of spicing, but beware of chillies in vinegar – they can blow your head off!

Mushroom Roast ~ *UK*

This recipe was suggested by my friend Julia. It is a great centrepiece for a vegetarian Christmas. It is delicious served hot with Onion and Juniper Gravy (page 151) or cold with a salad.

Preparation time:
30 minutes

Cooking time:
40–45 minutes

SERVES 4–6

1 medium onion, chopped
2 tbsp olive oil
½ each green, red and yellow pepper, de-seeded and chopped
450g/1lb brown mushrooms, sliced
175g/6oz wholemeal breadcrumbs
1 tbsp dried mixed herbs, or 2 tbsp fresh herbs of your choice

1 large free-range egg, beaten
sea salt and black pepper to taste
paprika to taste
115g/4oz vegetarian Cheddar, grated
1 large or 2 small tomatoes, sliced

In a large saucepan, sauté the onion in the oil for 5 minutes. Stir in the chopped peppers and cook for a further 5 minutes, stirring occasionally.

Add the sliced mushrooms and cook gently until they soften for 1 or 2 minutes. Remove from the heat, stir in the breadcrumbs and herbs and mix well. Fold in the beaten egg. Season with salt and pepper and a little paprika to taste.

Spoon the mixture into a well-greased 900g/2lb loaf tin and press down well. Sprinkle the grated cheese over the top and bake at 180°C/350°F/gas 4 for 40–45 minutes. Arrange the tomato slices on top for the last 15 minutes of baking.

Allow the roast to cool for at least 20 minutes before lifting it out carefully and slice using a very sharp knife.

SIDE DISHES

Chargrilled Vegetables **v** *Spain*

SERVES 4

1 medium aubergine
2 medium courgettes
1 yellow pepper, de-seeded and
  quartered
2 medium potatoes, washed, cut into
  chunks and blanched
4–6 tbsp olive oil

4 large flat mushrooms, sliced
2 medium tomatoes, quartered
Classic Vinaigrette made with garlic
  (page 151)
chopped parsley or coriander to garnish
sea salt and black pepper to taste

*Preparation time:
30–40 minutes*

Cut the aubergine and courgettes into chunky batons. Grill and skin the pepper.

Put the aubergine, courgettes, yellow pepper and potatoes into a large bowl and drizzle a little oil over them and toss, then repeat until they are well covered.

Pre-heat the grill to maximum. Put the vegetables on a roasting tray in a single layer. Grill, and turn until they brown nicely all over.

Remove the roasting tray, add the mushrooms and tomatoes and toss well. Return to the grill for a further 10 minutes or until the vegetables are tender and well grilled. Put them on to a plate to cool.

When the vegetables have cooled, season to taste, toss them in sufficient garlic vinaigrette to moisten and serve at room temperature, sprinkled with a little chopped parsley or coriander.

Mangetout with Ginger and Garlic **v** *China*

SERVES 2–3

1 tsp cornflour
5 tbsp vegetable stock (page 32)
40g/1½oz butter or margarine
2 cloves garlic, chopped finely
2 thin slices fresh ginger, shredded
  finely

225g/8oz mangetout, trimmed
sea salt and black pepper to taste
1 tbsp soy sauce
sesame seeds, toasted (page 60)

*Preparation time:
15 minutes*

Mix the cornflour with the stock. In a large frying pan melt the butter or margarine and add the garlic and ginger. Stir-fry for 1 minute over a medium heat.

Add the mangetout and coat well with the butter or margarine. Season to taste with salt and pepper, add the stock mixture and soy sauce and cook for 2–3 minutes, until the mangetout turn bright green. Serve garnished with sesame seeds.

Chilli Spring Greens

Chilli Spring Greens ∨ *Kenya*

SERVES 4-6

Preparation time:
25 minutes

900g/2lb kale or spring greens, washed and chopped
4 tbsp water or vegetable stock
2 tbsp groundnut oil
1 medium onion, chopped finely
1 medium tomato, skinned and chopped finely

1 chilli pepper, de-seeded and chopped finely
sea salt and black pepper to taste
4 tbsp ground peanuts
2 tsp fresh lemon juice

Put the chopped greens into a large saucepan with the water or stock and cook gently, covered, for 10 minutes until tender.

Meanwhile, in a medium frying pan, heat the groundnut oil and sauté the chopped onion, tomato and chilli for 2–3 minutes.

Place the sautéd onion mixture on the greens, but do not stir it in. Season with salt and pepper to taste. Sprinkle the ground peanuts on top. Cover and steam gently for a further 10 minutes.

Add the lemon juice, check the seasoning and serve.

Oven Potato Chips v *UK*

SERVES 3–4

450g/1lb potatoes, cut into medium
  chips
3 tbsp olive oil

1 tbsp soy sauce
garlic powder (optional)
sea salt

Preparation time:
10 minutes

Cooking time:
20–25 minutes

In a large bowl, toss the potatoes in the olive oil and soy sauce, and sprinkle them with garlic powder.

Transfer to a baking tray and roast at 220°C/425°F/gas 7 for 25–30 minutes, turning from time to time until golden brown. Sprinkle the chips with salt and pepper and serve.

Yam Chips v *USA*

SERVES 3–4

450g/1lb yam, peeled
chilli powder or cayenne pepper

oil for deep-frying
sea salt

Preparation time:
20 minutes

Cut the yam into slices and then into chips. Put them into a medium saucepan, cover with cold water and bring to the boil. Cook for 5 minutes, then drain and dry on kitchen paper. Sprinkle with a good pinch of chilli powder or cayenne pepper.

Pour 5–7.5-cm/2–3-inches of oil into a medium saucepan and place on a medium to high heat. The oil is ready when a cube of bread browns immediately. Cook the chips for 6–8 minutes until they are golden and crisp. Drain on kitchen paper, sprinkle with salt and serve at once.

Marinated Tofu Chips v *China*

SERVES 4

450g/1lb firm tofu, cut in 1-cm/
  ½-inch batons
5 tbsp water
2 cloves garlic
150ml/¼ pint red wine vinegar
dash of red wine (optional)

150ml/¼ pint soy sauce or tamari
3 cloves
2 tbsp unrefined sugar
sea salt and black pepper to taste
groundnut oil for deep-frying

Preparation time:
20 minutes
(plus
marinating time)

Drain the tofu for 10 minutes on a clean tea towel to remove excess moisture.

Combine the remaining ingredients in a small saucepan and simmer slowly for 5–10 minutes. Place the tofu in a bowl, pour the marinade over it and leave in a cool place for a minimum of 1 hour or refrigerate for up to 24 hours.

Pour 5–7.5-cm/2–3-inches of oil into a medium saucepan and place on a medium to high heat. The oil is ready when a cube of bread browns immediately. Carefully lower the drained tofu into it, a batch at a time and fry until golden brown all over. Drain on kitchen paper, and serve at once.

Potato and Onion Gratin v *France*

SERVES 4

Preparation time:
20 minutes

Cooking time:
1½ hours

450g/1lb waxy potatoes, peeled and
  sliced thinly
350g/12oz onions, sliced thinly
1 clove garlic, halved

sea salt and black pepper to taste
750ml/1¼ pints dairy or soya milk, or
  single dairy or soya cream
40g/1½oz butter or margarine

Rinse the potatoes in cold water to wash out some of the starch, and dry thoroughly.
Rub a deep earthenware dish with a cut clove of garlic. Arrange alternate layers of
potato and onion in the prepared dish, seasoning generously between each layer.

Pour the milk or cream over them, and dot the top with little pieces of butter or
margarine. Bake at 160°C/325°F/gas 3 for 1½ hours, turning the heat up to
200°C/400°F/gas 6 for the last 10 minutes to brown and crisp the top.

Special Mashed Potato v *UK*

SERVES 4

Preparation time:
30 minutes

5 medium floury potatoes, peeled and
  quartered
2 tbsp dairy or soya milk or cream
1 tbsp butter or margarine
1 tbsp finely chopped spring onion

2 tsp freshly chopped herbs of your
  choice
sea salt and black pepper to taste

In a medium saucepan, boil the potatoes in lightly salted water for about 20 minutes
until tender, then drain.

Add the milk or cream and butter or margarine, mash the potatoes, then whisk
them with a fork until they are creamy, fluffy and lump-free.

Fold in the spring onion and herbs and season to taste with salt and pepper.

Potatoes with Lemon v *Greece*

SERVES 4

Preparation time:
15 minutes

Cooking time:
1 hour

900g/2lb medium potatoes, peeled
juice of 1 lemon
sea salt and black pepper to taste

85g/3oz butter or margarine
150ml/¼ pint hot water

Halve the potatoes lengthwise, then quarter them lengthwise to make wedges.
Arrange them in a medium ovenproof dish and pour the lemon juice over them.
Season, and dot with the butter or margarine.

Pour the water into the dish and bake uncovered at 190°C/375°F/gas 5 for about
1 hour until tender, basting at least twice during cooking.

Herby Potato Cakes v *UK*

SERVES 4–6

900g/2lb potatoes, peeled and cubed
50g/2oz butter or margarine
2 tbsp freshly chopped mixed herbs,
   e.g. parsley, chives, sage, thyme,
   rosemary, marjoram, or 1 tbsp mixed
   dried herbs

freshly grated nutmeg
2 tbsp dairy or soya cream
sea salt and black pepper to taste
vegetable oil for shallow-frying

Preparation time:
45 minutes

In a medium saucepan, cook the potatoes in boiling water for 15 minutes or until they are tender. Drain.

Melt the butter or margarine in the same pan and mix in the herbs. Cook very gently for 2–3 minutes.

Return the potatoes to the pan. Heat gently and mash thoroughly until fluffy. Season well with salt, pepper and some grated nutmeg and stir in the cream.

Allow to cool before shaping into thin cakes with floured hands. Heat 5-mm/ ¼-inch of oil in a large frying pan until it is hot. Fry the cakes until they are golden brown on each side. Serve at once.

Potato Fry v *India*

SERVES 4

3 large potatoes, peeled
1 tsp chilli powder
4 tbsp freshly chopped coriander (or
   flat-leaf parsley if preferred)

sea salt and black pepper to taste
4–6 tbsp vegetable oil for frying

Preparation time:
40–50 minutes

Grate the potatoes and soak them in cold water for 10 minutes before draining and drying them thoroughly on a clean tea towel. Put them in a medium bowl, mix with the chilli powder and coriander or parsley, and season to taste with salt and pepper.

Heat 2–3 tablespoons of the oil in a large frying pan and spread the potato mixture over it. Press down to form a thick pancake and fry over a medium heat until the base is browned and crisp, about 10–15 minutes.

Turn the potato fry over carefully, add 2–3 tablespoons of oil to the pan, and cook the other side until it is crisp and golden, for 10–15 minutes. Serve, cut in wedges.

TIP
An easy way to flip the fry is to turn it out, upside down, on to a plate the same size as the frying pan, then add a little fresh oil to the pan and slide it off the plate and back into the pan.

Candied Sweet Potatoes v *Caribbean*

SERVES 6

Preparation time:
10 minutes

Cooking time:
40–45 minutes

900g/2lb sweet potatoes, washed and
   sliced
175g/6oz unrefined muscovado sugar

grated zest of ½ lemon
50g/2oz butter or margarine, melted

Mix all the ingredients together in a greased medium ovenproof dish. Cover with
foil and bake at 200°C/400°F/gas 6 for 40–45 minutes, until the sweet potatoes
are tender.

Hawaiian-style Sweet Potatoes v *Hawaii*

SERVES 3–4

Preparation time:
45 minutes

Cooking time:
20 minutes

450g/1lb sweet potatoes, washed
1 banana, peeled and cubed
2 tbsp unrefined brown sugar

juice of ½ grapefruit
2 tbsp desiccated coconut

In a medium saucepan, boil the sweet potatoes in their skins for 30–35 minutes, until
tender. Allow to cool, then peel and cube. Mix with the banana, and spoon into a
medium casserole dish.

In a small saucepan, dissolve the sugar in the grapefruit juice over a gentle heat, and
pour it over the sweet potato and banana. Bake at 190°C/375°F/gas 5 for 20 minutes.

Sprinkle the coconut over the top and place the dish under a pre-heated grill for a
minute until it is lightly browned.

Caramelized Onions v *France*

SERVES 4

Preparation time:
1 hour

25g/1oz butter or margarine
1kg/2lb mixed white and red onions,
   sliced

3 tbsp unrefined sugar
sea salt and black pepper to taste
a little cold water

In a large saucepan, melt the butter or margarine and toss the onion slices in it until
evenly coated.

Sprinkle the sugar over the onions, season with salt and pepper and barely cover
with cold water.

Bring to the boil and simmer, uncovered, until the water evaporates – 30–40
minutes. Stir towards the end of the cooking time to prevent the onions from
burning. Serve warm.

Fine Beans with Almonds **V** *France*

SERVES 2-3

225g/8oz fine green beans
25g/1oz flaked almonds, toasted
  (page 70)

2–3 tbsp freshly chopped dill
1 tsp olive oil
sea salt and black pepper to taste

Preparation time:
10–15 minutes

Steam the beans for 4–5 minutes until *al dente*. Stir in the remaining ingredients and serve.

Grilled Courgettes with Red Sauce **V** *Italy*

SERVES 2–3

3 tbsp olive oil
2 medium courgettes, cut into 1-cm/
  ½-inch slices
2 large tomatoes, seeded and diced

3 cloves garlic, thinly sliced
1 red pepper, roasted, skinned and
  diced
sea salt and black pepper to taste

Preparation time:
15 minutes

Put 2 tablespoons of oil in a medium bowl and add the courgettes. Toss them with your hands to coat them thoroughly with oil.

Grill the courgettes on a pre-heated griddle or under a grill until lightly charred, 4 minutes on each side.

Heat the remaining oil in a small frying pan. When hot, carefully add the tomatoes and garlic. When the garlic starts to colour, add the red pepper. Spoon the tomato mixture over the courgettes and season to taste.

Button Onions with Cream and Thyme **V** *Spain*

SERVES 4

700g/1lb 9oz button onions
25g/1oz butter or margarine
1 tbsp freshly chopped thyme
350ml/12fl oz vegetable stock (page
  32)

125ml/4fl oz dairy or warmed soya
  cream
sea salt and black pepper to taste

Preparation time:
40–45 minutes

To peel the onions, submerge them in a bowl of boiling water for 5 minutes, drain and allow to cool slightly before making a cut in the bottom of each one with a sharp knife. The onions will then pop out of their skins easily.

In a medium frying pan, melt the butter or margarine and sauté the onions, shaking the pan occasionally, for 8–10 minutes until they start to brown. Add the thyme and stock, and bring to the boil. Then reduce the heat and simmer, uncovered, for 15 minutes or until the onions are cooked but still slightly crisp.

Pour in the cream and heat through. Check the seasoning and serve.

Top to bottom:
Fine Beans with Almonds,
Grilled Courgettes with
Red Sauce, Button Onions
with Cream and Thyme

Grilled Squash with Herb Butter v *USA*

SERVES 4–6

700g/1lb 9oz squash, peeled
  and de-seeded
2 tbsp olive oil
sea salt and black pepper to taste
115g/4oz butter or margarine, melted
1 shallot, chopped finely

1 medium clove garlic, crushed
2 tsp fresh lemon juice
¼ tsp finely grated lemon zest
2 tbsp freshly chopped parsley
2 tsp freshly chopped thyme
2 tsp freshly chopped marjoram

Preparation time:
30–40 minutes

Cut the squash into 1-cm/½-inch slices. Brush them with olive oil and season with salt and pepper. Grill the squash – preferably on a charcoal grill – for 5–6 minutes on each side until tender.

Meanwhile, make the herb butter by combining the remaining ingredients in a small saucepan and heating them through gently. Drizzle the herb butter over the squash and serve.

Winter Squash Baked with Leeks v *USA*

SERVES 4

450g/1lb squash, peeled, de-seeded and
  cubed
450g/1lb leeks, washed, trimmed and
  chopped roughly

2 cloves garlic, chopped finely
4 tbsp olive oil
sea salt and black pepper to taste
8–12 fresh sage leaves

Preparation time:
25 minutes

Cooking time:
20 minutes

In a large saucepan toss the squash, leeks, garlic and olive oil over a medium heat for 5–6 minutes. Season to taste with salt and pepper.

Put the vegetables into a medium baking dish and add the sage leaves. Cover with foil and bake at 220°C/425°F/gas 7 for about 20 minutes, until the vegetables are tender.

Spicy Okra v *India*

SERVES 4

300ml/½ pint coconut milk
350g/12oz okra, trimmed
2 tbsp vegetable oil
2 small dried chillies, left whole

1 clove garlic, crushed
1 tsp each cumin seeds, mustard seeds
  and poppy seeds
fresh lemon juice to taste

Preparation time:
15 minutes

In a medium saucepan heat the coconut milk gently and simmer the okra in it until tender, about 7–8 minutes.

Heat the oil in a small frying pan and brown the chillies, garlic and spices until the seeds begin to spit. Remove the whole chillies and pour over the okra. Add a squeeze of lemon juice. Serve hot or cold.

Marrow with Dill and Soured Cream

~ *Hungary*

Preparation time:
40 minutes

SERVES 4

700g/1lb 9oz marrow, peeled,
  de-seeded and grated
sea salt
25g/1oz butter or margarine
1 small onion, chopped
2 tbsp plain flour

2 tbsp freshly chopped dill
175ml/6fl oz vegetable stock (page 32)
150ml/¼ pint soured cream
2 tsp white wine vinegar
1 tsp unrefined caster sugar

Place the grated marrow in a colander and sprinkle lightly with salt. Allow it to stand for 30 minutes.

In a large saucepan, melt the butter or margarine and add the onion. Cover the pan and cook the onion over a gentle heat, until it is soft and translucent, about 5–6 minutes, stirring occasionally.

Sprinkle the flour over the onions and stir well. Add the dill and mix again, then stir in the stock. Simmer and stir until the sauce thickens, about 3–4 minutes.

Squeeze the excess moisture from the marrow then add the sauce. Stir in the soured cream, then the vinegar and sugar and cook for a further 5 minutes before serving.

Roasted Mushrooms with Peperonata **v** *Italy*

Preparation time:
45 minutes

Cooking time:
15 minutes

SERVES 6

700g/1lb 9oz flat mushrooms, sliced
  thickly
125ml/4fl oz olive oil
2 large white onions, sliced finely
2 cloves garlic, crushed
1 bay leaf
3 each red and yellow peppers,
  de-seeded and cut into strips

450g/14oz tinned chopped tomatoes,
  drained
sea salt and black pepper to taste
4 tbsp red wine vinegar
2 tbsp freshly chopped basil

Arrange the mushrooms on a baking tray and drizzle liberally with half of the olive oil. Roast at 200°C/400°F/gas 6 for 15 minutes.

Heat the remaining oil in a large pan and sauté the onions until golden and translucent, about 10 minutes. Add the garlic and bay leaf, and continue to cook for 3 minutes. Add the peppers and cook for a further 5–10 minutes, stirring continuously until just tender. Then add the tomatoes and seasonings. Simmer uncovered for 10 minutes until the juices from the tomatoes have evaporated.

Remove the bay leaf and stir in the vinegar and basil. Leave to cool, then stir in the mushrooms and serve.

Glazed Carrots with Honey and Sesame Seeds v *USA*

Preparation time:
15–20 minutes

SERVES 4

450g/1lb carrots, peeled and cut into batons
50g/2oz butter or margarine
2 tbsp honey (or maple syrup for vegans)

pinch of salt
300ml/½ pint water
1 tbsp sesame seeds, toasted (page 60)

Put the carrots into a medium pan with half the butter or margarine and honey or maple syrup, and a pinch of salt, then add the water. Bring to the boil, uncovered, and cook rapidly until the water has all but evaporated and the carrots are tender, about 8 minutes.

Add the remaining butter or margarine and honey or maple syrup and cook until a thick syrup forms to coat the carrots, 3–4 minutes longer. Serve sprinkled with the sesame seeds.

Spicy Sweetcorn v *Mexico*

Preparation time:
20 minutes

SERVES 2–3

1 tbsp olive oil
1 red pepper, diced
2 tsp mild chilli powder
350g/12oz sweetcorn kernels
4 spring onions, chopped finely

2–3 tbsp freshly chopped coriander (or flat-leaf parsley if preferred), chopped
juice of 1 lime
sea salt and black pepper to taste

In a medium saucepan heat the oil and add the red pepper and chilli powder. When the oil sizzles, add the corn and cook for 5 minutes. Add the remaining ingredients and season to taste.

Oven-roasted Vegetable Chips with Whole Garlic v *USA*

Preparation time:
15–20 minutes

Cooking time:
20–25 minutes

SERVES 3–4

1 large parsnip
1 large turnip
1 large beetroot
1 small fennel bulb

1 medium celeriac, peeled
3–4 tbsp olive oil
12–16 cloves garlic, unpeeled
sea salt and black pepper to taste

Scrub the root vegetables thoroughly but leave them unpeeled. Cut them into chips. Transfer to a large bowl and toss with the olive oil and garlic until well coated. Season with salt and pepper.

Spread the vegetables evenly on a baking tray in a single layer. Roast at 220°C/425°F/gas 7 for 20–25 minutes until they are crisp and tender, turning from time to time so that they brown all over. Serve hot.

Top to bottom:
Glazed Carrots with Honey and Sesame Seeds, Spicy Sweetcorn, Oven-roasted Vegetable Chips with Whole Garlic,

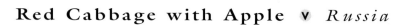

Red Cabbage with Apple v *Russia*

SERVES 4–6

25g/1oz butter or margarine
1 medium onion, diced
1 medium red cabbage, core discarded,
   and sliced (about 550g/1lb 4oz
   prepared weight)
300ml/½ pint water

2 tbsp vinegar
1 tbsp unrefined brown sugar
sea salt and black pepper to taste
2 medium dessert apples, cored, peeled
   and chopped

Preparation time:
1 hour 20 minutes

In a large saucepan, melt the butter or margarine and sauté the onion for about 5 minutes. Stir in the sliced cabbage and toss for a further 2 minutes.

Add the water, vinegar, brown sugar, salt and pepper and apples. Bring the mixture to the boil, reduce the heat, cover and simmer for 1 hour.

Crispy Fried Seaweed v *China*

SERVES 4

225g/8oz spring greens, outer cabbage
   leaves or curly kale, rinsed and dried
vegetable oil for deep-frying

soy sauce to taste
chilli powder (optional)
2 tbsp sesame seeds, toasted (page 60)

Preparation time:
15 minutes

Lay the leaves on top of each other and roll them up tightly. Using a sharp knife, slice the rolls crosswise into very thin strands, then separate the strands.

Heat 5–7.5-cm/2–3-inches of oil in a wok or large saucepan. The oil is ready when a cube of bread browns immediately. Add a small handful of the greens at a time, standing well back because they spit ferociously as they hit the oil. Allow them to fry for about 1 minute until they shrink and darken, but do not let them overcook and burn. Remove with a slotted spoon, and drain thoroughly on kitchen paper.

Repeat this process until all the greens have been cooked. Season with soy sauce to taste and an optional pinch of chilli powder. Serve sprinkled with sesame seeds.

Minted Peas v *UK*

SERVES 4–6

8–12 sprigs of fresh mint, leaves
   removed and chopped, stalks reserved
450g/1lb fresh or frozen peas

15g/½oz butter or margarine
sea salt and black pepper to taste

Preparation time:
25–30 minutes

Pour 5cm/2 inches of boiling water into a medium saucepan, add the mint stalks, simmer for 5 minutes then remove. Add the peas to the water. Cook frozen peas according to the packet instruction; if you are using fresh peas, cook them until tender, for 8–10 minutes then drain.

Stir in the mint leaves and butter or margarine and season to taste.

Swede Mash with Horseradish v *UK*

Preparation time: 30 minutes

SERVES 4

450g/1lb swede, peeled and cubed
5 spring onions, sliced
2 tsp grated horseradish

grated zest and juice of ½ lemon
4 tbsp single dairy or soya cream
sea salt and black pepper to taste

In a medium saucepan, boil the swede for about 15 minutes until tender. Drain. Mash thoroughly with the remaining ingredients and serve.

Cauliflower with Dijon Mustard Sauce v *France*

Preparation time: 20 minutes

SERVES 3–4

350g/12oz cauliflower, cut into florets
50g/2oz butter or margarine
50g/2oz plain flour

3 tbsp Dijon mustard
600ml/1 pint dairy or soya milk
sea salt and black pepper to taste

Steam or boil the cauliflower until tender for about 5 minutes.

Meanwhile, melt the butter or margarine in a small saucepan, add the flour and combine thoroughly. Cook gently for 1 minute, stirring. Add the mustard and stir until it is mixed through, then pour in the milk gradually, whisking continuously until it thickens and forms a smooth sauce. Bring to the boil and simmer gently for 4–5 minutes.

Put the cauliflower in a medium ovenproof dish, pour the sauce over the top and put the dish under a pre-heated grill for 5 minutes until the top is lightly golden.

Leeks with Balsamic Dressing v *Italy*

Preparation time: 20–30 minutes

SERVES 4

8 small leeks, halved
4 tbsp olive oil
1 tbsp balsamic vinegar

1 tsp wholegrain mustard
sea salt and black pepper to taste

Steam or boil the leeks until tender, for about 8–10 minutes. Drain thoroughly.

Whisk the oil, vinegar and mustard together and season to taste.

Serve the leeks drizzled with the balsamic dressing.

Lemon Spinach v *Spain*

SERVES 2–3

400g/14oz spinach leaves, rinsed
1 tsp lemon juice
1 tsp grated lemon zest

¼ tsp ground nutmeg
1 tbsp olive oil
sea salt and black pepper to taste

Preparation time:
10 minutes

Put the spinach in a large saucepan and allow it to wilt over a high heat for 1–2 minutes. Drain and gently squeeze out excess water.

Combine the remaining ingredients, toss with the spinach and season to taste. Serve hot or cold.

Seeded Cabbage v *Germany*

SERVES 2

225g/8oz Savoy cabbage, shredded
25g/1oz butter or margarine
1 tbsp cumin seeds

2 tbsp mustard seeds
1 tsp cider vinegar
sea salt and black pepper to taste

Preparation time:
15 minutes

Steam or boil the cabbage until slightly tender, for about 3–4 minutes, then drain. In a large frying pan, heat the butter or margarine and seeds. When the first mustard seeds pop, add the cabbage, vinegar and seasoning, and cook, stirring, for 5 minutes over a medium heat.

Brussels Sprouts with Sesame Seeds v *UK*

SERVES 3–4

450g/1lb Brussels sprouts, trimmed
3 tbsp sesame oil
25g/1oz sesame seeds

2 tsp paprika
juice of ½ lemon or 1 lime
sea salt and black pepper to taste

Preparation time:
20 minutes

Put the prepared sprouts into a medium saucepan. Cover with boiling water and cook until tender, for about 6 minutes. Drain the sprouts.

Meanwhile combine the oil, seeds and paprika in a small saucepan over a medium heat. When the seeds begin to colour, remove the pan from the heat. Add the lemon or lime juice, season to taste and pour the sauce over the sprouts.

Brussels Sprouts with Chestnuts v *UK*

Preparation time:
25 minutes

SERVES 6-8

900g/2lb Brussels sprouts, trimmed
50g/2oz butter or margarine
225g/8oz tinned whole chestnut

6-8 vegetarian bacon slices, cut into
  thin strips (optional)
sea salt and black pepper to taste

Put the prepared sprouts in a large saucepan. Cover with boiling water and cook until tender, for about 6 minutes. Drain and return to the pan.

In a medium frying pan, melt the butter or margarine and fry the bacon pieces until crisp. Stir in the chestnuts and cook for 1–2 minutes until warmed. Add to the sprouts, season to taste and serve.

Stir-fried Parsnip and Turnip v *UK*

Preparation time:
20-25 minutes

SERVES 3-4

2 tbsp vegetable oil
225g/8oz parsnips, peeled and
  sliced thinly
225g/8oz turnips, peeled and
  sliced thinly

1 tbsp soy sauce
2 cloves garlic, crushed
sea salt and black pepper to taste

Heat the oil in a wok or large frying pan over a high heat and toss the vegetables in it for several minutes until they are well coated, beginning to soften and lightly browned, about 7–8 minutes.

Add the remaining ingredients, toss well, reduce the heat and cook for a further 1–2 minutes. Check the seasoning and serve immediately.

Mediterranean-style Green Beans v *Spain*

SERVES 2–3

350g/12oz runner or green beans,
  sliced lengthwise
2 tbsp freshly chopped basil

1 clove garlic, chopped
sea salt and black pepper to taste
2 tbsp chopped chives, to garnish

Preparation time:
6–8 minutes

Steam or boil the beans until tender, for about 6–8 minutes.

Toss the beans with the basil and garlic, season to taste with salt and pepper and garnish with chives.

Green Beans with Red Onion v *Belgium*

SERVES 2–3

225g/8oz green beans
1 small red onion, finely chopped
25ml/1fl oz white wine vinegar

1 tbsp balsamic vinegar
75ml/2½fl oz olive oil
sea salt and black pepper to taste

Preparation time:
5–6 minutes

Steam or boil the beans until tender, for about 5–6 minutes. Combine the remaining ingredients and pour over the beans. Season to taste.

Special Fried Rice v *Thailand*

SERVES 6

350g/12oz long-grain rice
2 tbsp groundnut oil
1 medium onion, chopped
1–2 tsp soy sauce
2 tsp chilli bean sauce
3 tbsp tomato purée

3 tbsp chopped spring onions
2 tsp freshly chopped coriander (or
  flat-leaf parsley if preferred)
4 large free-range eggs, beaten
  (optional)

Preparation time:
15–20 minutes

Cook the rice according to packet instructions.

Heat a wok or large frying pan and add the oil. When it is hot, add the chopped onion and stir-fry for 2–3 minutes. Add the rice and continue to toss for 3 minutes.

Add the remaining ingredients, except the eggs, and stir-fry over a high heat for 5 minutes. Fold in the beaten eggs, stirring continuously, until they set (omit the eggs for vegans). Serve at once.

Fragrant Coconut Rice v *Thailand*

SERVES 4–6

Preparation time:
30–35 minutes

2 tbsp groundnut oil
1 medium red onion, chopped
2 tsp turmeric
280g/10oz long-grain rice
425ml/15fl oz coconut milk
450ml/¾ pint vegetable stock
  (page 32)

2 whole cloves
7.5-cm/3-inch cinnamon stick
2 bay leaves
85g/3oz broken cashews or almonds,
  toasted (page 70)
soy sauce to taste

TIP

Use a heavy-
bottomed saucepan
because the rice can
burn easily.

Heat the oil in a large saucepan or flameproof casserole dish, add the onion and stir-fry for 2 minutes.

Add the turmeric and stir for a few moments, then stir in the rice for a further 2–3 minutes. Add the coconut milk and the stock and bring to the boil. Stir in the cloves, cinnamon and bay leaves, then reduce the heat as low as possible and cover. Cook undisturbed for 18–20 minutes or until the rice is thoroughly cooked.

Fold in the nuts and add soy sauce to taste. Leave the dish to stand for 5 minutes to allow the flavours to develop.

Fragrant Coconut Rice

Saffron Rice v *India*

SERVES 4

Preparation time:
35–40 minutes

25g/1oz butter or margarine
1 small onion, chopped finely
2 cloves garlic, chopped finely
450ml/¾ pint vegetable stock (page 32)

large pinch of saffron strands, to taste
sea salt and black pepper to taste
175g/6oz basmati rice

In a medium saucepan, heat the butter or margarine, add the onion and garlic, cover the pan and cook gently until soft and translucent, about 10 minutes.

Heat the stock, stir in the saffron and season to taste.

Toss the rice into the onion mixture and stir for 1–2 minutes. Then add the hot stock and allow the mixture to simmer, covered, for about 15 minutes.

Remove from the heat, season to taste, and leave to stand for 5 minutes before serving, to allow the flavours to develop.

Bulgar and Pine Nut Pilaf v *Africa*

SERVES 4

Preparation time:
40–45 minutes

2 tbsp olive oil
1 medium onion, chopped
2 cloves garlic, chopped
1 tsp turmeric, or a pinch of
  saffron strands
½ tsp ground cinnamon
1 green chilli, de-seeded and chopped
750ml/1¼ pints vegetable stock
  (page 32)

225g/8oz bulgar wheat, rinsed under
  cold water and drained
15g/½oz butter or margarine
50g/2oz pine nuts
2 tbsp freshly chopped parsley

In a large saucepan, heat the oil and fry the onion, covered, until tender, for about 8 minutes, stirring occasionally. Add the garlic, turmeric or saffron, cinnamon and chilli, and fry for 1 minute.

Add the stock, bring to the boil and add the bulgar wheat to the pan. Cover and simmer for about 15 minutes, until the stock has absorbed and the bulgar is tender.

Meanwhile, melt the butter or margarine in a small saucepan, add the pine nuts and brown gently, tossing until golden all over. Add to the bulgar wheat with the chopped parsley, stir with a fork and serve.

SAFFRON

Saffron used to demand a price higher than gold and is still an expensive spice today. It consists of the stamens of the saffron crocus, which have to be gathered manually, and picked out by hand. Over 250,000 flowers must be picked to produce 500g/1lb of saffron. It is cultivated in many Mediterranean countries, although Spain is the main producer. Some cheaper powdered saffron may be an adulterated form, merely a coloured and flavoured mixture, so where you can, use the tiny thread-like stamens – they are intensely strong and you need only a pinch to flavour a large quantity of food.

SAUCES AND SUNDRIES

Sweet and Sour Chilli Dipping Sauce v *China*

SERVES 4

6 tbsp white or rice vinegar
4 tbsp unrefined brown sugar
1 tbsp soy sauce

1 small red chilli, de-seeded and
   chopped very finely
½ tsp grated fresh ginger

Preparation time:
10 minutes

In a small saucepan, boil the vinegar with the sugar until it has slightly thickened, about 5 minutes. Add the soy sauce and the chilli, then stir in the ginger.

Ginger Dipping Sauce v *Vietnam*

SERVES 4

3 spring onions, chopped finely
1 tsp grated fresh ginger
1 clove garlic, crushed

2 tbsp soy sauce
2 tbsp sesame oil
2 tbsp cold water

Preparation time:
5 minutes

Whisk all the sauce ingredients together in a small bowl.

Chunky Tomato Sauce with Harissa v *Morocco*

SERVES 3–4

2 tbsp olive oil
1 large onion, chopped finely

400g/14oz tinned chopped tomatoes
1–2 tsp harissa paste (see below)

Preparation time:
20–25 minutes

Heat the oil in a medium saucepan. Add the onion, cover and cook over a gentle heat for about 10 minutes until softened.

  Add the tomatoes with their juices and simmer uncovered for 5 minutes. Stir in the harissa paste and mix well. Taste the sauce and add more harissa if you would like it really spicy. Heat through just before serving.

HARISSA PASTE

This hot spicy condiment is what gives Moroccan cooking its fiery kick. You can buy it quite easily now in shops or delis, in small jars or cans or you can make it yourself. To do this, you will need 50g/2oz of dried chillies, 2 garlic cloves, and a pinch of salt and 2 tbsp of olive oil. Simply place the chillies in a bowl and pour over enough hot water to cover. Leave to stand until the water is cold – at least 2 hours. Drain the chillies and place in a food processor or blender with the garlic. Process to a thick paste, similar in consistency to tomato purée. Rub through a sieve, being careful not to get any on your hands. Spoon the mixture into a clean, glass jar. Cover the surface with a little oil to seal it, screw the lid on tightly and it will keep in the fridge for up to 3 months.

Garlic Dipping Sauce v *Thailand*

Preparation time:
15–20 minutes

SERVES 4

225g/8oz unrefined sugar
150ml/¼ pint water
150ml/¼ pint white vinegar
3 cloves garlic, crushed

1 tsp sea salt
1 tsp chilli powder
1 tbsp freshly chopped coriander

Mix the sugar, water, vinegar, garlic and salt in a medium saucepan. Bring the mixture to the boil, stirring to dissolve the sugar. Then turn the heat down and simmer until the sauce thickens slightly, about 10–15 minutes.

Remove the pan from the heat, and add the chilli powder and coriander. Allow the mixture to cool a little before serving.

Skorthalia (THICK GARLIC SAUCE) v *Greece*

Preparation time:
10–15 minutes

SERVES 4

85g/3oz crustless white bread, soaked
  in water and squeezed out
3 cloves garlic, crushed
1 tbsp white wine vinegar

pinch of sea salt
6 tbsp olive oil
25g/1oz ground almonds or walnuts
2 tbsp cold water (optional)

Place the damp bread in the blender; add the garlic, vinegar and a pinch of salt, and blend until smooth. While the blender is still running, add the olive oil in a thin stream. Then add the nuts and blend again. Add the water or a little more oil if necessary to thin out the sauce: it should be the consistency of thick cream.

Yoghurt with Fresh Mint v *Lebanon*

Preparation time:
35 minutes
(plus 30 minutes
standing time)

SERVES 4–6

4 tbsp fresh finely chopped mint
300ml/½ pint plain dairy or
  soya yoghurt

lemon juice to taste
sea salt and black pepper to taste

Mix the chopped mint into the yoghurt and season to taste with a little lemon juice, salt and pepper. Allow the sauce to stand for at least half an hour, so that the flavour of the mint permeates the yoghurt.

Tahini Citrus Sauce v *Greece*

Preparation time:
5 minutes
(plus 30 minutes
standing time)

SERVES 4–6

6 tbsp tahini
3 tbsp fresh orange juice

6 tbsp lemon juice

Combine the ingredients and allow the sauce to stand for at least half an hour.

Cranberry Sauce v *USA*

SERVES 8

450g/1lb fresh or frozen cranberries
1 large thin-skinned orange (Seville if available)

170g/6oz unrefined caster sugar

Cooking time:
10 minutes

Wash the cranberries and pick them over for stems. Put them in a liquidiser. Slice both ends off the orange, but leave the rest of the peel on. Cut the orange into small pieces and remove the pips. Place the orange pieces in the liquidiser with the cranberries. Add the sugar and purée to an even consistency. Chill in the fridge before serving.

Satay Sauce v *Thailand*

SERVES 4

175g/6oz crunchy (wholenut) peanut butter
1–2 cloves garlic, crushed

1 tsp chilli powder
175ml/6fl oz vegetable stock, warmed (page 32)

Preparation time:
5 minutes

Mix the first three ingredients together in a small bowl and slowly stir in the stock.

Rocket and Herb Pesto ~ *Italy*

SERVES 2–4

4 tbsp freshly chopped rocket
4 tbsp freshly chopped coriander
2 tbsp freshly chopped flat-leaf parsley
1 tsp chopped red chilli
4 tbsp olive oil
1 tbsp sesame oil

1 tbsp vegetable stock (page 32)
1 tbsp pine nuts, chopped finely
85g/3oz vegetarian Pecorino cheese, grated
sea salt and black pepper to taste

Preparation time:
10 minutes

Combine the ingredients in a medium bowl until well mixed. Serve with pasta or gnocchi (potato dumplings).

Pesto Sauce ~ *Italy*

SERVES 2

6 tbsp freshly chopped fresh basil
2 large cloves garlic, crushed
85g/3oz pine nuts or walnuts, chopped

50g/2oz vegetarian Parmesan, grated
150ml/¼ pint olive oil
sea salt and black pepper to taste

Preparation time:
5 minutes

In a medium bowl mix the basil, garlic, nuts and cheese. Stir in the olive oil and season to taste.

Green Curry Paste v *Thailand*

Preparation time:
25 minutes

MAKES 8 TBSP

2 long green chillies, de-seeded
  and chopped
6 small green (bird's eye) chillies,
  chopped and de-seeded
1 stalk lemon grass, chopped
3 small shallots, chopped
4 cloves garlic, chopped
2.5-cm/1-inch piece of galangal,
  chopped, or fresh ginger

4 tsp freshly chopped coriander
1 tsp ground coriander
½ tsp ground cumin
½ tsp ground white or black pepper
grated zest of 2 small limes or 1 tsp
  chopped kaffir lime leaves
1 tsp sea salt

In a small liquidiser (or using a pestle and mortar) blend all of the ingredients
together to form a smooth paste.

Roasted Red Pepper Sauce v *Spain*

Preparation time:
45 minutes

SERVES 6

5 red peppers
2 large tomatoes
1–2 tbsp olive oil

2–3 tbsp crème fraîche or warmed soya
  cream
sea salt and black pepper to taste

Put the peppers and tomatoes on a baking tray and roast them at 200°C/400°F/
gas 6 for 20–30 minutes, turning from time to time until the peppers have blackened
and the tomatoes have cooked.

Cool the peppers in a paper bag for 10 minutes, then peel off the skins, core and
de-seed them. Skin the tomatoes. Put the peppers and tomatoes in the blender with
the olive oil. Blend to a purée. Pour into a small saucepan and add the crème fraîche
or soya cream. Stir well, season to taste and heat through to serve.

Special Gravy v *UK*

Preparation time:
25 minutes

SERVES 3–4

2 tbsp olive oil
1 medium onion, chopped finely
115g/4oz mushrooms, chopped small
2 tsp tomato purée
2 tbsp vegetarian gravy granules

450ml/¾ pint vegetable stock (page
  32) or water
sea salt and black pepper to taste

In a medium saucepan, heat the oil and cook the onion until golden brown, 5–6
minutes. Stir in the mushrooms and cook until soft, a further 5 minutes, stirring.
Add the tomato purée.

Sprinkle the gravy granules into the mixture, stir well, then add the stock or water
slowly, stirring continuously. Bring to the boil, then simmer gently for 5 minutes.
Season to taste with salt and pepper before serving.

Tomato Coulis v *UK*

MAKES 600ML/1 PINT

450g/1lb ripe plum tomatoes, skinned
  and chopped (page 121)
1 large onion, chopped
4 medium sticks celery, chopped

paprika to taste
1 tbsp soy sauce (optional)
2 tsp unrefined sugar
1 tbsp freshly chopped rosemary

*Preparation time
15-20 minutes*

Put the tomatoes, onion and celery into a large saucepan and simmer, uncovered for
5 minutes, stirring continuously. Add the rest of the ingredients and simmer, covered,
for a further 10-15 minutes, stirring occasionally, until the vegetables have softened.
Blend in a liquidiser or force through a sieve to make a smooth sauce.

Curry Sauce v *India*

SERVES 3–4

1 small onion, chopped
2 tsp vegetable oil
1 tsp curry powder
1 tsp tomato purée
150ml/¼ pint vegetable stock
  (page 32)

150ml/¼ pint dairy or warmed
  soya milk
1 tsp cornflour
juice of ½ lemon
2–3 tsp mango chutney

*Preparation time:
15 minutes*

In a medium saucepan fry the chopped onion in the oil until soft. Add the curry
powder and tomato purée and stir gently. Add the vegetable stock, milk and
cornflour and bring to the boil, stirring continuously until it thickens. Add the lemon
juice and mango chutney and simmer for a further 5 minutes. Strain through a sieve
or blend in a food processor before serving.

Salsa Verde v *Mexico*

SERVES 6

2–3 jalapeño chillies, stems and seeds
  removed, fresh or preserved
350g/12oz tomatilloes or green
  (unripe) tomatoes, skinned and
  chopped (page 121)
1 medium onion, chopped small

1 tsp unrefined sugar
4 tbsp freshly chopped coriander leaves
  (or flat-leaf parsley if preferred)
juice of 1 lime
sea salt and black pepper to taste

*Preparation time:
15 minutes*

Finely chop the chillies, discarding the seeds if using fresh.

  In a medium saucepan, cook the tomatoes, onions and chillies in 1-cm/½-inch
water over a medium heat for about 5 minutes until softened. Leave to cool, stir in
the remaining ingredients and season to taste.

Salsa v *Mexico*

Preparation time:
5–10 minutes

SERVES 4

400g/14oz tinned chopped tomatoes, or
  450g/1lb fresh, skinned (page 121)
  and diced
1 small or ½ medium red onion, chopped
2 mild green chillies, chopped finely

2 tsp lemon juice
pinch of unrefined sugar if required
2 tbsp fresh finely chopped coriander (or
  flat-leaf parsley if preferred)

In a medium bowl mix all the ingredients together and season to taste.

Onion and Juniper Gravy v *UK*

Preparation time:
40–45 minutes

SERVES 4–6

2 small onions, chopped
25g/1oz butter or margarine
125ml/4fl oz red wine
3 tbsp vegetarian gravy granules

12 juniper berries, crushed finely
600ml/1 pint vegetable stock (page 32)
sea salt and black pepper to taste

In a medium saucepan, sauté the onions in the butter or margarine until golden. Add the wine and bring to the boil.

Add the gravy granules and juniper berries and slowly stir in the stock. Simmer uncovered for 10 minutes, stirring occasionally. Season to taste with salt and pepper.

Classic Vinaigrette v *France*

Preparation time:
*5 minutes
(plus 30 minutes
standing)*

SERVES 4

1–2 tsp fine or grainy Dijon mustard
2 tbsp fresh lemon or lime juice or
  2 tbsp wine vinegar, balsamic vinegar
  or cider vinegar

6 tbsp olive oil
crushed garlic to taste (optional)
sea salt and black pepper to taste

In a small bowl, mix the mustard with the lemon or lime juice or vinegar. Whisk in the olive oil gradually. Stir in the garlic if you are using it and season to taste with salt and pepper.

Creole Vinaigrette v *USA*

Preparation time:
5 minutes

MAKES 225ML/8FL OZ

60ml/2fl oz red wine vinegar
1 tbsp mustard
1 clove garlic, crushed
1–2 tsp Cajun Spice Mix (page 152)

½ tsp cayenne pepper
Tabasco to taste
sea salt and black pepper to taste
175ml/6fl oz olive oil

Combine all the ingredients except the oil in a small bowl. Gradually whisk in the oil until the mixture thickens. It will keep in a covered jar in the fridge for up to ten days.

Spicy Pecan Mix v *USA*

MAKES APPROXIMATELY 450G/1LB

450g/1lb shelled pecan pieces
2 tbsp vegetable oil
1 tbsp Cajun Spice Mix (below)
1–2 tsp sea salt

50g/2oz each sunflower seeds and
  pumpkin seeds
2 tbsp tamari or soy sauce

Preparation time:
10 minutes

Mix all the ingredients together in a roasting tin and roast at 180°C/350°F/gas 4 for 20 minutes. Allow the nuts to cool. This mix will keep in an airtight container for several weeks. Use them as a salad topping or serve with drinks.

Cajun Spice Mix v *USA*

MAKES APPROXIMATELY 50G/2OZ

15g/½oz paprika
10g/¼oz black pepper

2–3 tsp cayenne pepper or to taste
1 tbsp garlic powder

Preparation time:
5 minutes

Mix the spices together in a small bowl. Store in an airtight container.

Dumplings v *Germany*

MAKES 8

115g/4oz self-raising flour
50g/2oz vegetarian suet
1 tbsp dried mixed herbs, or freshly
  chopped basil

sea salt and black pepper to taste
water to bind

Preparation time:
25–30 minutes

Mix the flour with the suet, herbs and some salt and pepper, then add enough cold water to form soft manageable dough. Shape the dough into eight dumplings and cook them in simmering stock or soup for 20–25 minutes.

Croûtons v *France*

SERVES 4

3 medium slices day-old bread
4–5 tbsp olive oil

garlic powder to taste

Preparation time:
20–25 minutes

Cut the crusts off the bread and cut the slices into small dice. Place them in a medium bowl, drizzle with the oil, sprinkle with garlic powder and toss well.

   Roast the croûtons at 200°C/400°F/gas 6 for 15–20 minutes, turning occasionally until they are golden and crisp.

Chestnut Stuffing 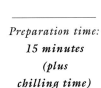 *UK*

SERVES 6–8

400g/14oz tinned chestnut purée
3 sticks celery, chopped finely
1 medium onion, chopped finely
85g/3oz wholemeal breadcrumbs

1 tbsp freshly chopped sage
1 tbsp dried mixed herbs
soy sauce to taste

In a medium bowl, mix all the ingredients thoroughly together.

Shape the stuffing into walnut-sized balls and place them evenly on a greased baking tray. Bake at 190°C/375°F/gas 5 for 20–25 minutes until crisp.

Preparation time:
10 minutes

Cooking time:
20–25 minutes

Herby Stuffing *USA*

SERVES 4–6

1 medium onion, chopped finely
6 small sticks celery, chopped
1 tbsp each freshly chopped parsley,
   sage and thyme
6 tbsp olive oil

small loaf of granary bread, diced
25g/1oz each roughly chopped pecans,
   cashews and brazil nuts
soy sauce or tamari to taste
a little stock or water to bind

In a medium bowl, combine all the ingredients.

Mix well, adding a little stock or water to moisten the mixture. Press the mixture into a greased loaf tin. Bake at 180°C/350°F/gas 4 for 30–40 minutes. Allow the stuffing to cool a little before turning it out. Serve cut into slices.

Preparation time:
15 minutes

Cooking time:
30–40 minutes

Easy Shortcrust Pastry

MAKES 275G/9OZ

175g/6oz plain flour
large pinch of fine sea salt

85g/3oz butter or margarine
3 tbsp ice cold water

Sift the flour and salt into a medium bowl and rub in the margarine, lifting the mixture to incorporate as much air as possible. When the mixture resembles fine breadcrumbs, bind it with water. Knead lightly on a floured surface until smooth. Wrap and chill for a minimum of 30 minutes before rolling out.

Preparation time:
15 minutes
(plus
chilling time)

Sweetcrust Pastry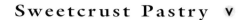

MAKES 350G/12OZ

225g/8oz plain flour
1 tbsp unrefined caster sugar
115g/4oz butter or margarine

½ tsp vanilla essence
3 tbsp ice cold water

Preparation time:
20 minutes
(plus
chilling time)

Sift the flour into a large bowl and stir in the sugar. Rub in the butter or margarine lightly until the mixture resembles fine breadcrumbs. Add the vanilla essence and bind with the water. Knead lightly on a floured surface. Wrap and chill for a minimum of 30 minutes before rolling out.

Crunchy Wholemeal Pastry V

Don't be put off by the unusual ingredients! This is a deliciously light and crunchy pastry that's worth a try even if you are not a vegan.

MAKES 350G/12OZ

225g/8oz wholemeal plain flour
  (organic if available)
115g/4oz margarine

25g/1oz sesame seeds
1 tbsp soy sauce
2 tbsp ice cold water

Preparation time
20 minutes
(plus
chilling time)

Place the flour in a large bowl. Rub the margarine into the flour until it resembles fine breadcrumbs. Stir in the sesame seeds and then bind the dry mixture with the soy sauce and cold water. Knead lightly on a floured surface and then wrap and chill for a minimum of 30 minutes before rolling out.

DESSERTS, CAKES AND BISCUITS

Spiced Fruit Filo Parcels V *Greece*

These deliciously moist and sticky little pastries were inspired by the traditional Greek baklava. Serve them with Greek yoghurt.

MAKES APPROXIMATELY 15

115g/4oz sultanas
3–4 tbsp Amaretto liqueur or orange juice
225g/8oz macadamias, pistachios or almonds, toasted (page 70) and chopped
1 tsp ground cinnamon
2 tsp ground allspice

1 tbsp vanilla essence
175g/6oz sheets filo pastry cut into 15-cm/6-inch square
50g/2oz margarine, melted
450g/1lb unrefined sugar
300ml/½ pint water
juice and pared zest of 1 lemon
1 cinnamon stick

Place the sultanas in a medium bowl, pour the Amaretto or orange juice over them and leave to soak for a couple of hours.

Mix in the chopped nuts, spices and vanilla essence.

Brush a sheet of filo with melted margarine. Spoon a heaped tablespoon of the nut mixture into the centre, fold in the edges and roll it up. Brush the top with more margarine and place on a greased baking tray. Repeat this process until you have used up all the nut mixture.

Bake at 180°C/350°F/gas 4 for 40 minutes until golden brown.

Meanwhile, make the syrup by dissolving the sugar in the water over low heat, then boil it with the lemon juice and zest and cinnamon stick for 5–6 minutes, until it is thin and sticky. When the pastries have cooked, pour the syrup over them through a sieve. Leave them to cool completely, turning occasionally so that they are evenly soaked in the syrup. Serve cold.

Fruit Flan V *Belgium*

SERVES 6–8

23-cm/9-inch flan tin, lined with 1 quantity Sweetcrust Pastry (page 154)
50g/2oz plain chocolate, melted
600ml/1 pint crème pâtissière (page 163)
115g/4oz green or black seedless grapes, washed

2 bananas, peeled and sliced
115g/4oz each raspberries and redcurrants, washed
3–4 tbsp apricot jam, warmed and sieved

Bake the pastry case blind (page 161) and leave it to cool. Brush the base and sides with chocolate and chill until set.

Spread the crème pâtissière over the bottom of the pastry case. Arrange the prepared fruit decoratively in concentric circles on top.

Brush the warmed apricot jam over the top of the fruit. Allow it to cool completely before serving.

Preparation time:
25 minutes
(plus
soaking time)

Cooking time:
40 minutes

TIP
A lemon zester is a wonderfully useful piece of equipment. Small and simple, cheap and easily available, it scrapes the zest finely and easily and works far better than a grater, which tends to dig into the pith.

Preparation time:
45 minutes

Sopapillas (SWEET TORTILLA FRITTERS) ∨ *Mexico*

Preparation time:
15 minutes

These little Mexican doughnuts can be served drizzled with maple syrup or honey and dusted with sugar and cinnamon.

SERVES 4 (MAKES 8 LARGE SOPAPILLAS)

225g/8oz plain flour
1 tsp salt
2 tsp baking powder
2 tbsp margarine

175ml/6fl oz cold water
vegetable oil for deep-frying
unrefined caster or icing sugar and
   honey or maple syrup to serve

Sift the flour, salt and baking powder into a large bowl. Rub in the margarine until crumbly. Work in the water to form a pastry-like dough.

Knead lightly on a floured board until smooth, then roll out to a round 3mm/ ⅛ inch thick. Cut into 8 triangles.

Pour 5–7.5cm/2–3 inches of oil into a medium saucepan and place on a medium to high heat. The oil is ready when a cube of bread browns immediately. Deep-fry the dough triangles a few at a time until they puff up and turn a light golden colour, turning them so that they cook evenly, for about 3–4 minutes. Remove carefully from the oil and drain on kitchen paper.

Serve dusted with sugar or drizzled with honey or maple syrup.

Apple Pancakes ∨ *The Netherlands*

Preparation time:
30–40 minutes

Dutch pancakes are legendary for their size and golden crispness, with whole restaurants devoted to savoury and sweet *pannekoeken*. For these smaller fruit pancakes use a tart apple such as Granny Smith or Bramley.

SERVES 4–6

3 large apples, peeled, cored and
   coarsely grated
150ml/¼ pint lemon juice
175g/6oz plain flour
2 tsp baking powder
pinch of sea salt
175ml/6fl oz dairy or soya milk

175ml/6fl oz water
2 tbsp vegetable oil
2 tsp unrefined sugar
vegetable oil for shallow-frying
unrefined caster sugar and ground
   cinnamon to serve

Marinate the apples in the lemon juice for 20 minutes, then drain thoroughly.

Sift the flour, baking powder and salt into a large bowl. Stir in the milk to make a smooth batter, then beat in the water, oil and sugar. Finally, fold in the drained apples.

Heat 5mm/¼ inch of oil in a large frying pan until it is hot. Spoon in 3–4 tablespoons of batter at a time to make each pancake. Fry until crisp and golden on each side, 1–2 minutes. Drain on kitchen paper and serve sprinkled with sugar and cinnamon.

Rhubarb Fool ∨ *Ireland*

When selecting your rhubarb, choose young, pink stems rather than older ones, which will be thick, stringy and acidic.

Preparation time:
30 minutes

SERVES 4

700g/1lb 9oz rhubarb, cut into small
   pieces
225g/8oz unrefined light muscovado
   sugar
¼ tsp ground cloves
2 tbsp fresh orange juice

½ tsp orange zest
1½ tsp vanilla essence
300ml/½ pint double cream, lightly
   whipped or 200g/7oz silken tofu and
   5 tbsp soya cream, blended together
Grand Marnier (optional)

Place the rhubarb, sugar, cloves and orange juice with the zest in a medium saucepan and cook it gently for 10–15 minutes, stirring occasionally until it softens.

Remove from the heat and add the vanilla essence. Allow to cool, then chill it in the fridge until completely cold.

Combine the tofu mixture or whipped cream with Grand Marnier to taste. Fold this into the cold rhubarb so that it has a marbled effect. Spoon the fool into individual glasses and chill in the fridge.

TIP
Never eat raw rhubarb or the leaves, which are poisonous. It keeps in the fridge for only a day or two before it becomes limp.

Ice-cream Cake ∨ *USA*

Use any combination of your favourite ice-cream or sorbet.

Preparation time:
25 minutes

SERVES 8

1 Lemon Sponge Cake (page 180)
3 flavours (and colours) of soya ice-
   cream or sorbet, about 175g/6oz of
   each

2 quantities of Icing (page 180)

Line an 18-cm/7-inch deep cake tin with greaseproof paper so that it overhangs the edges. Cut the sponge into 1-cm/½-inch slices and press them into the base and around the sides of the lined tin.

Fill the centre with ice-cream and/or sorbet scoops. Press down hard so that as much as possible fits in. Place the cake tin in the freezer for a minimum of 1 hour.

When the cake is firm, turn it upside down on to a plate, remove the tin and peel off the greaseproof paper. Spread the top and sides with icing and freeze for a further 20 minutes. Serve immediately.

Rhubarb Fool

Coconut Rice Pudding v *Thailand*

The coconut milk gives this unusual rice pudding an exotic flavour. It is particularly good served with a swirl of mango coulis made by puréeing two ripe mangoes with 25g/1oz unrefined icing sugar.

Preparation time:
40 minutes

SERVES 5–6

115g/4oz long-grain or jasmine rice
400ml/14fl oz tin coconut milk
850ml/1½ pints dairy or soya milk
115g/4oz unrefined sugar
pinch of sea salt

1 tsp vanilla essence
115g/4oz desiccated coconut
shredded coconut to decorate

Mix the rice, coconut milk, milk, sugar and a pinch of salt in a large saucepan. Bring to the boil and stir continuously, then simmer gently for about 25 minutes, stirring frequently.

Stir in the vanilla and desiccated coconut and simmer for a further 5 minutes.

Serve warm or cold with a swirl of mango coulis and sprinkle with shredded coconut which has been toasted in a dry frying pan over a gentle heat.

Honey Pudding v *Greece*

This is a good way of using up left-over bread. As an alternative to honey, you can serve the pudding with maple syrup for vegans.

Preparation time:
25 minutes

SERVES 4

12 slices bread, cut into rounds
300ml/½ pint dairy or soya milk,
    plus 5 tbsp
3 tbsp vegetable oil
3 tbsp cornflour

½ tsp baking powder
pinch of sea salt
85g/3oz margarine
115g/4oz shelled pistachios, chopped
warmed honey or maple syrup, to serve

Soak the rounds of bread in 300ml/½ pint milk for a few seconds until they are soft but not mushy. Set aside.

In a medium bowl, combine the oil, cornflour, baking powder, remaining 5 tablespoons of milk and a pinch of salt and beat well. Melt the margarine in a large frying pan over a medium heat. Dip the rounds of bread into the batter and fry until they are crisp and golden on each side, for about 1–2 minutes.

Serve warm, sprinkled with chopped pistachios and honey or maple syrup poured over them.

Grandma's Apple Pie ~ *USA*

Two things that are quintessentially American are baseball and home-baked apple pie, which is often served at Thanksgiving as an alternative to pumpkin pie.

Preparation time:
25 minutes

Cooking time:
35–40 minutes

SERVES 8

175g/6oz butter or margarine, softened
175g/6oz low-fat cream cheese
350g/12oz plain flour
900g/2lb apples, peeled, cored and
    sliced thinly

2 tbsp ground cinnamon
5–6 tbsp unrefined sugar, to taste,
    depending on the sweetness of the
    apples
2 tbsp lemon juice

In a medium bowl beat the butter or margarine and cream cheese together until smooth. Work in the flour to make a soft dough. Divide into two balls, wrap and chill for a minimum of one hour.

Mix the sliced apples with the cinnamon, sugar and lemon juice, reserving a little sugar and cinnamon.

On a lightly floured surface roll out one pastry ball and use to line a deep 25cm/ 10 inch pie dish. Bake the pastry blind (see below).

When the pastry has cooled, fill it with the apples, piling them higher in the centre.

Roll out the other pastry ball thinly and gently lay it over the top. Press the edges together, trim excess pastry then mark the edges with a fork and prick the top of the pie several times.

Mix the reserved cinnamon and sugar together and sprinkle the mixture over the top of the pie. Bake at 190°C/375°F/gas 5 for 35–40 minutes, until the pastry is golden brown and set and the apples have cooked.

TIP

If the pastry begins to brown too early, cover the pie loosely with foil.

BAKING BLIND

Baking blind, which partly cooks the pastry, will ensure that it stays crisp under a liquid filling. Cover the pastry closely, including the rim, with cooking foil; to prevent it from rising. Weigh it down with baking beans (dried butterbeans are perfect). Bake in a pre-heated oven at 200°C/400°F/Gas 6, for 10–12 minutes (slightly less time if making, small individual cases). Remove the foil and bake for a further 5 minutes or until the pastry starts to colour.

Pecan Roulade ~ *USA*

This is a sophisticated version of a Swiss roll which is made with a pecan nut sponge base. It is easier to make than you might think.

Preparation time:
50 minutes

Cooking time:
20–25 minutes

SERVES 8

6 large free-range eggs, separated
175g/6oz unrefined caster sugar, plus 2
  tbsp
350g/12oz pecans, chopped finely
1 tsp baking powder

300ml/½ pint double cream
1 tsp vanilla essence
225g/8oz raspberries or strawberries,
  washed and trimmed
unrefined icing sugar to decorate

Grease a 23 x 33-cm/9 x 13-inch Swiss roll tin and line it with non-stick baking parchment.

In a large bowl, whisk the egg yolks with 175g/6oz of sugar until the mixture turns pale yellow. Fold in the pecans and the baking powder.

Whisk the egg whites until stiff. Stir 2–3 tablespoons of the whites into the nut mixture, then gently fold in the rest.

Spread the mixture on to the prepared baking tray, level the surface and bake at 180°C/350°F/gas 4 for 20–25 minutes until just firm to the touch. Cover with a lightly dampened tea towel and leave for 15 minutes, then chill in the fridge for a further 15 minutes.

Whip the cream with the vanilla essence and the extra 2 tablespoons of sugar until thick. Finally, gently fold in the berries.

Carefully turn the chilled sponge out on to the tea towel. Gently peel off the paper.

Spread the whipped cream on to the pecan cake and roll it up with the aid of the tea towel. Dust with icing sugar before serving.

Crème Pâtissière v *France*

MAKES 600ML/1 PINT

Preparation time:
5–10 minutes

4 tbsp cornflour
8 tbsp unrefined caster sugar
pinch of sea salt
500ml/18fl oz soya milk

2 tbsp vegetable oil
1 tbsp vanilla essence
2 tbsp Grand Marnier (optional)

In a medium bowl, combine the cornflour, sugar and a pinch of salt with sufficient cold milk to make a paste.

In a medium saucepan, heat the remaining milk to boiling point, and gradually pour it into the paste, stirring continuously. Return it to the saucepan and heat it gently over a low heat, stirring, until it thickens. Let it bubble very gently for 2–3 minutes to cook the cornflour.

Finally, stir in the vegetable oil, vanilla and Grand Marnier, and leave the crème to cool before using.

Pecan Roulade

Mississippi Mud Pie ~ *USA*

It is unclear how this pie got its name, as it isn't originally from Mississippi. Perhaps someone thought the rich layers of chocolate mousse and caramel on a biscuit base looked like the mud flats along America's most famous river!

Preparation time:
60 minutes
(plus chilling time)

SERVES 12

2 tbsp coffee granules
200ml/⅓ pint condensed milk
175g/6oz unsalted butter, melted
175g/6oz digestive biscuits, crushed
175g/6oz ginger biscuits, crushed
225g/8oz plain chocolate, broken into
 squares
2 large free-range eggs, separated

150ml/¼ pint double cream
115g/4oz margarine
115g/4oz unrefined sugar
2 tsp golden syrup
2 medium bananas
chocolate curls to decorate
2 tsp cocoa powder

Grease a 20-cm/8-inch cake tin with a removable base. In a small bowl, mix the coffee granules into the condensed milk, stir well and put to one side to stand.

Mix the melted butter with the crushed biscuits. Press the mixture into the tin so that it covers the bottom and sides evenly. Place it in the fridge to chill for a minimum of 30 minutes.

Melt the chocolate in a bowl over a pan of hot water. Remove from the heat and allow to cool slightly, then beat in the egg yolks and the cream. Whisk the egg whites until stiff and fold them into the chocolate mixture. Pour the filling into the prepared biscuit case and chill for at least two hours.

Place the condensed milk and coffee mixture in a medium saucepan with the margarine, sugar and golden syrup. Melt the ingredients slowly over a low heat. When melted, increase the heat to medium, stirring continuously. Bring to a gentle boil and cook for a further 5 minutes, stirring continuously and taking care that the mixture doesn't stick to the base of the pan and burn.

You can test it by dropping a little of the mixture in some cold water on a saucer: if it stays in a soft ball, it is ready. Remove the pan from the heat and allow the sauce to cool, beating it now and again.

Spread the sauce over the chocolate mixture in the tin and chill for a minimum of 3 hours.

Remove the pie carefully from the tin. Decorate it with circles of sliced bananas, cover with the chocolate curls and dust with sifted cocoa powder.

Fruit Soufflés with Coulis ~ *France*

These deliciously light soufflés are served with a fruit coulis and/or crème fraîche.

Preparation time:
15 minutes

Cooking time:
12–15 minutes

SERVES 6

15g/½oz butter, melted
unrefined icing sugar for dusting
700g/1lb 9oz prepared mixed fruit,
    such as raspberries, strawberries,
    apricots, peaches, bananas, kiwi,
    blackberries

1 tsp vanilla essence
1–2 tbsp unrefined icing sugar
6 large free-range eggs, separated
6–7 tbsp unrefined caster sugar

Lightly butter six individual soufflé dishes and sprinkle them with a little icing sugar.

Purée the prepared fruit, and mix in the vanilla essence. To make the coulis, take half this mixture, stir in the icing sugar and chill.

Whisk the egg whites until stiff. Gradually whisk in the sugar until the mixture becomes thick and glossy.

Beat the egg yolks and mix with the remaining fruit purée. Stir in 2–3 tablespoons of the egg whites, then fold in the rest gently. Pour the mixture into the prepared dishes and bake at 200°C/400°F/gas 6 for about 12–15 minutes or until the soufflés have risen and lightly browned. Serve immediately.

TIP

It is possible to sieve the purée to get rid of the berry pips, but I prefer to leave them in.

Key Lime Pie ~ *USA*

This wonderfully refreshing dessert is a local speciality in the Florida Keys, where particularly tart limes grow semi-wild.

Preparation time:
30 minutes
(plus freezing time)

SERVES 6

175g/6oz digestive biscuits
2 tbsp unrefined caster sugar
50g/2oz butter or margarine, melted
3 large free-range egg yolks, beaten
400g/14oz tin condensed milk

juice of 3 large limes
finely grated zest of 1 large lime
150ml/¼ pint double cream, whipped
slices of lime to decorate

Crush the biscuits to fine crumbs in a large bowl. Stir in the sugar, then mix thoroughly with the melted butter or margarine. Press the mixture into a greased 20-cm/8-inch flan tin and chill for at least 30 minutes in the fridge.

In a medium bowl, beat the egg yolks until creamy. Slowly beat in the condensed milk and stir in the lime juice and zest. Pour the mixture into the flan tin and freeze until firm, for 2–3 hours.

When ready to serve, remove the pie from the freezer and decorate it with whipped cream and lime slices. It does not freeze hard and is delectable eaten this cold.

Panna Cotta with Raspberry Coulis ~ *Italy*

SERVES 6

450g/1lb prepared raspberries
175g/6oz unrefined icing sugar
1.2 litres/2 pints double cream

2 vanilla pods, split
pared zest of 2 lemons
50ml/2fl oz brandy (optional)

Preparation time:
1 hour 15 minutes
(plus chilling time)

Purée the berries in a blender with 25g/1oz of the sugar, then strain the purée through a sieve to remove the seeds. Divide this coulis among six dessert bowls.

Pour 850ml/1½ pints of the cream into a wide, shallow pan, add the vanilla pods and lemon zest, and bring to the boil slowly over a low heat. Simmer until the mixture has reduced by half, about 45 minutes.

Remove the lemon zest and allow the mixture to cool. Then remove the vanilla pods and squeeze the seeds into the cream.

Whip the remaining cream with the remaining icing sugar until thick and fold it into the cooled vanilla cream. Stir in brandy to taste and pour the cream over the coulis in the bowls. Chill for at least 2 hours before serving. Decorate with extra fruit.

Coconut Pie ~ *Caribbean*

When we were recording the *Tug of War* album, we spent a lot of time in the Caribbean and this unusual pudding soon became one of my favourites.

SERVES 8

23-cm/9-inch flan tin lined with 1
   quantity Sweetcrust Pastry (page 154)
3 tbsp cornflour
85g/3oz unrefined caster sugar
400ml/14fl oz dairy or soya milk

15g/½oz butter or margarine
1 tsp vanilla essence
2 tsp ground allspice
85g/3oz desiccated coconut
2 large free-range eggs, separated

Preparation time:
15 minutes

Cooking time:
15–20 minutes

Bake the pastry case blind (page 161) and leave it to cool. Meanwhile, mix the cornflour with 50g/2oz of the sugar and sufficient cold milk to make a paste. Warm the remaining milk with the butter or margarine in a small pan. Gradually stir the warmed milk into the paste. Return the mixture to the pan and cook gently until it thickens, stirring continuously.

Add the vanilla, allspice and coconut, and stir for 2 minutes. Remove from the heat and allow to cool slightly before beating in the egg yolks.

Whisk the egg whites until stiff, then whisk in the remaining sugar until they become thick and glossy. Stir 2 tablespoons of the egg whites into the coconut mixture, then fold in the rest. Pour the filling into the prepared pastry case and bake at 180°C/350°F/gas 4 for 15–20 minutes until the pie has browned lightly and set in the centre.

Panna Cotta
with Raspberry Coulis

Naughty Nougat Cake ~ *Norway*

This is a cake that my friend, Helge, made for me. He usually makes it for special occasions like birthdays, weddings and Christmas, but it is amazing how many other excuses to make it we can find!

Preparation time:
30 minutes

Cooking time:
45 minutes

SERVES 10–12

300g/10½oz ground almonds
350g/12oz unrefined icing sugar
6 large free-range egg whites
50g/2oz butter or margarine
50g/2oz dark chocolate, broken into
  pieces

30ml/1fl oz strong black coffee
2 large free-range egg yolks
2 tbsp shredded almonds, toasted (page
  70), to decorate

Sift the almonds and 300g/10½oz of the icing sugar into a large bowl.

Whisk the egg whites until stiff. Stir a quarter of them into the almond and sugar mixture, then gently fold in the rest.

Put the mixture into a well-greased 23-cm/9-inch round cake tin and bake at 180°C/350°F/gas 4 for about 45 minutes. Allow to cool, then turn out on to a plate.

Meanwhile, make the topping by creaming the butter or margarine with the remaining sugar until it turns a thick and creamy pale yellow.

Melt the chocolate with the coffee in a bowl over a pan of hot water. Remove the bowl from the heat and place in the fridge for 10 minutes. Next, beat the egg yolks into the butter and sugar until it is pale and creamy, then add the chilled chocolate and coffee mixture and beat until smooth.

When the cake is completely cool, decorate it with the topping. If you are confident enough to use a piping bag do so, but if not, simply spread the topping over the top and sides of the cakes using a palette knife and finish it off with a sprinkling of toasted, shredded almonds.

Naughty Nougat Cake

Exotic Fruit Platter V *India*

This dish takes advantage of the many types of interesting and exotic fruit now available. It is so simple to assemble but with a bit of imagination and creativity makes an exquisite finale to any dinner party. Served with a delicious vegan crème anglaise, it is a winner for vegans and non-vegans alike.

SERVES 6–8

2kg/4lb 6oz selection of prepared fruit, such as pineapple, passion fruit, physalis, watermelon, starfruit
85g/3oz unrefined caster sugar

300ml/½ pint water
juice of ½ lime
2 tsp vanilla essence

Preparation time:
30 minutes

Arrange the prepared fruit decoratively on a large serving plate.

In a small saucepan, dissolve the sugar in the water over a medium heat, stirring, then turn it into a light syrup by boiling for 3–4 minutes. Stir in the lime juice and vanilla essence.

Allow the syrup to cool before pouring it over the prepared fruit. Chill for at least 10 minutes before serving with a jug of crème anglaise (see below).

Crème Anglaise V *France*

MAKES APPROXIMATELY 450ML/15FL OZ

500ml/16fl oz soya milk, plus 2 tbsp
1 vanilla pod, split
85g/3oz unrefined caster sugar

3 tbsp cornflour
2 tbsp vegetable oil

Preparation time:
15 minutes

In a medium saucepan, warm the 500ml/16floz of soya milk with the vanilla pod. Do not allow it to boil. In a medium bowl, mix the caster sugar, cornflour, vegetable oil and remaining milk to a paste. Pour the warmed milk into the paste stirring continuously.

Return this mixture to the saucepan and cook gently over a medium heat, stirring continuously. When the sauce begins to thicken and turn creamy, reduce the heat. Don't allow the mixture to boil: it should just bubble gently for 5 minutes more. Remove the vanilla pod and squeeze the seeds into the crème anglaise.

Pour it into a jug and serve warm or cold.

Exotic Fruit Platter with
Crème Anglaise

Celebration Pudding ~ *UK*

This is a traditional steamed fruit pudding with an exotic slant. Serve with cream or with the Crème Anglaise (page 170).

*Preparation time:
25 minutes
(plus soaking time)*

*Cooking time:
2 hours*

SERVES 6

115g/4oz dried mango slices
115g/4oz dried figs
115g/4oz shredded vegetarian suet
115g/4oz self-raising flour
115g/4oz breadcrumbs
115g/4oz unrefined light soft brown
  sugar
2 tsp ground cinnamon
2 tsp ground ginger

115g/4oz glacé pineapple wedges
50g/2oz glacé cherries, quartered
2 large free-range eggs, beaten
6 tbsp dairy or soya milk
1 large banana, mashed
3 tbsp brandy, plus extra for serving
grated zest and juice of 1 lime
1 tbsp molasses or black treacle

Cover the mango slices and figs with boiling water and soak them for an hour. Drain, chop and set aside.

Grease a 1.2-litre/2-pint pudding basin and place a small round of greaseproof paper in the bottom.

Put all the dry ingredients in a large bowl. Stir in all the fruit, except the banana, then beat in the eggs, milk, banana, brandy, lime zest and juice and the molasses or black treacle. Mix well.

Spoon the mixture into the pudding basin, cover it with greaseproof paper and kitchen foil and secure tightly with string.

Place the pudding in a large saucepan and fill it up to halfway with boiling water. Steam for 2 hours, replenishing the pan with hot water as necessary.

Turn the pudding out of the basin. Just before serving, pour extra brandy over the top, set it alight with a match and bring it flaming to the table. This should be done with great care.

Tarte Tatin ∨ *France*

Preparation time:
25 minutes,
(plus chilling time)

Cooking time:
30–35 minutes

This apple flan was created by the Tatin sisters at the Hôtel Terminus Tatin in Lamotte-Beuvron, a small village near Paris. It is traditionally baked with the pastry on top of the fruit and turned upside down before serving.

SERVES 6

PASTRY
200g/7oz plain flour
25g/1oz unrefined caster sugar
¼ tsp sea salt
¼ tsp baking powder
¼ tsp ground allspice
85g/3oz butter or margarine
3–4 tbsp water

FILLING
225g/8oz unrefined caster sugar
150ml/¼ pint water
900g/2lb dessert apples, cored and
   sliced
85g/3oz butter or margarine
1 tbsp lemon juice
½ tsp grated lemon zest
2 tbsp malt extract

To make the pastry, sieve the flour, sugar, salt, baking powder and allspice into a large bowl. Rub in the margarine, then stir in sufficient water to make a firm dough. Gather it carefully into a ball, wrap and chill in the fridge for 1 hour.

To make the filling, gently heat 175g/6oz of the sugar with the water until the sugar dissolves, then boil it until it turns a rich caramel colour. Carefully pour the caramel into a greased 25-cm/10-inch flan tin.

Gently cook and turn the apple slices in the margarine for 2–3 minutes, then add the lemon juice, zest, 50g/2oz of sugar and the malt extract and stir until it has dissolved.

Arrange the apples on top of the caramel in the flan tin. Roll the pastry out on a floured surface until it is large enough to cover the flan tin, allowing an extra 1-cm/½-inch all round. Lay it on top of the apples and press down with a fork.

Bake at 190°C/375°F/gas 5 for 30–35 minutes until the pastry is golden and crisp. Leave it to stand for 5–10 minutes before turning it upside down on to a plate. This is best done quickly and confidently over the sink. Serve warm or cold with pouring cream.

DESSERTS, CAKES AND BISCUITS

Pear Flan v *France*

There are numerous varieties of pear: choose your favourite one for this lovely flan.

Preparation time:
45 minutes,
(plus chilling time)

Cooking time:
25–30 minutes

SERVES 10

PASTRY

400g/14oz plain flour
½ tsp sea salt
50g/2oz unrefined icing sugar
½ tsp grated lemon zest
175g/6oz butter or margarine
100ml/3½fl oz water combined with 1
  tsp vanilla essence

BASE:

85g/3oz pecans, finely chopped
50g/2oz fresh breadcrumbs
50g/2oz unrefined light muscovado
  sugar
½ tsp ground cinnamon

FILLING

900g/2lb pears, cored and sliced
40g/1½oz unrefined caster sugar
50g/2oz margarine, diced
4 tbsp apricot jam, warmed and sieved
25g/1oz slivered almonds, toasted
  (page 70)

To make the pastry, sift the flour and salt into a large bowl and stir in the sugar and lemon zest. Rub in the butter or margarine lightly until the mixture resembles fine breadcrumbs. Bind the ingredients with the water. Knead lightly on a floured surface until smooth. Wrap and chill in the fridge for a minimum of 30 minutes before rolling out.

Roll out the pastry thinly to fit into a 30-cm/12-inch flan tin. Bake blind (page 161). Allow it to cool.

Combine the ingredients for the base in a medium bowl and sprinkle them over the bottom of the prepared pastry case before adding the pears.

Place the pears in concentric circles, overlapping them so that they spiral into the centre. Sprinkle the pears with sugar and dot with the margarine. Bake at 190°C/375°F/gas 5 for 25–30 minutes until the pears turn golden.

Glaze the surface of the flan with the warmed apricot jam and scatter the slivered almonds over the top. Serve warm or cold.

TIP

Squeeze lemon juice over the pear slices as you finish cutting them to prevent them discolouring.

Pear Flan

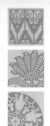

Warm Chocolate Soufflés with Bittersweet Sauce ~ *France*

Preparation time:
20 minutes

Cooking time:
15–20 minutes

Chocolate has been popular in France since the seventeenth century. Like wine, cocoa beans vary in quality and according to the fertility of the cultivation area. They are graded and tested by experts, many of whom are based in Bordeaux. These soufflés are a chocoholic's dream!

SERVES 6

115g/4oz unrefined caster sugar,
  plus 6 tsp
50g/2oz unsalted butter
175g/6oz plain chocolate, broken into
  pieces
pinch of sea salt

4 tbsp cocoa powder
1 tsp vanilla essence
4 medium free-range egg whites
unrefined icing sugar to decorate
1 quantity Bittersweet Sauce (see
  below)

Lightly butter six individual soufflé dishes and sprinkle a teaspoon of caster sugar into each one. Melt the butter in a medium saucepan and add the chocolate, a pinch of salt, the cocoa powder and 3 tablespoons of the sugar. Mix until smooth, then remove the pan from the heat and stir in the vanilla essence. Allow to cool slightly.

Whisk the egg whites until stiff, then whisk in the sugar until the mixture becomes thick and glossy. Stir 2–3 tablespoons of the egg whites into the chocolate mixture, then fold in the rest.

Spoon the chocolate mixture into the prepared dishes, filling each about two-thirds full. Place the dishes on a baking tray and bake at 200°C/400°F/gas 6 for 15–20 minutes, until the soufflés have puffed up and set lightly.

Dust with icing sugar and serve warm or cold.

Bittersweet Sauce v

Preparation time:
5–10 minutes

FOR 4–6

125ml/4fl oz strong black coffee
3 tbsp unrefined icing sugar
175g/6oz plain chocolate, broken into
  pieces

100ml/3½fl oz single dairy or warmed
  soya cream
1 tsp vanilla essence

Gently heat the coffee in a small saucepan over a low heat before adding the icing sugar, and continue to heat until it bubbles.

Remove the pan from the heat and add the chocolate. Stir until the chocolate has melted, then stir in the cream or soya cream and vanilla essence.

*Warm Chocolate Soufflés
with Bittersweet Sauce*

Non-dairy Crème Brulée ~ *France*

A friend of mine is lactose intolerant but adores crème brulée, so I experimented with this version at a dinner party. I hope you agree, as my friend did, that it's a real success.

Preparation time:
20 minutes
(plus chilling time)

SERVES 4–6

4 large free-range egg yolks
6–8 tbsp unrefined caster sugar

2 tsp vanilla essence
600ml/1 pint single soya cream

In a medium bowl, whisk the egg yolks with 2 tablespoons of caster sugar until they turn a thick and creamy pale yellow. Add the vanilla essence.

Put the cream into a medium saucepan and heat it over very low heat until just below boiling. Be careful that it doesn't burn.

Gradually pour the cream into the yolk mixture, beating with a whisk. Return the mixture to the pan and heat it gently, stirring with a wooden spoon over a very low heat, until it just thickens. This will take about 5 minutes. Pour the cream into individual soufflé dishes or ramekins and chill in the fridge until it has set.

Heat the grill to maximum. Sprinkle the top of each brulée evenly with 1 tablespoon of caster sugar. Place the dishes under the grill and allow the sugar to melt and brown a little, before removing and standing them in a cold place to allow the top to set hard.

TIP
Soya cream must be handled with loving care when cooking with it – do not be tempted to hurry!

Golden Syrup Sponge Pudding ⱽ *UK*

Serve this delectable pudding with as much golden syrup as your teeth and waistline can handle!

Preparation time:
20–25 minutes

Cooking time:
1¹/₂–2 hours

SERVES 6–8

9 tbsp golden syrup, plus extra to serve
175g/6oz plain flour
175g/6oz fresh breadcrumbs
115g/4oz shredded vegetable suet
50g/2oz unrefined caster sugar

2 tsp ground ginger
1¹/₂ tsp bicarbonate of soda
pinch of sea salt
¹/₂ medium banana, mashed
dairy or soya milk to thin

Grease a medium pudding basin and put 6 tablespoons of golden syrup in the bottom. In a large bowl, mix the dry ingredients.

In a medium bowl, combine the banana with the rest of the golden syrup and a little milk. Stir this into the dry mixture, adding more milk as required to bring it to a very soft dropping consistency.

Put the mixture into the basin, cover the top with greaseproof paper and secure it with string. Steam the pudding in a large pan of boiling water for 1¹/₂–2 hours, topping up the pan with hot water as necessary. Turn out on to a plate to serve.

Toffee Apples and Bananas ♥ *China*

These caramel-coated fruit pieces make a great finish to any meal, but especially an Oriental one.

Preparation time:
30–40 minutes

SERVES 4

25g/1oz plain flour
1 tbsp cornflour
pinch of sea salt
¼ tsp baking powder
75ml/2½fl oz dairy or soya milk
50ml/2fl oz water
1 tbsp sesame oil

groundnut oil for deep-frying
2 large firm apples, peeled, cored and
    cut into 8 thick wedges
2 large firm bananas, peeled and cut
    into 5-cm/2-inch chunks
225g/8oz unrefined caster sugar
2 tbsp sesame seeds

Sift the two flours, a pinch of salt and baking powder into a large bowl, and gradually beat in the soya milk, water and sesame oil to make a smooth, thick batter.

Pour 5–7.5-cm/2–3-inches of oil into a medium saucepan and place on a medium to high heat. The oil is ready when a cube of bread browns immediately. Dip the fruit into the batter in batches and deep-fry for about 2 minutes until golden. Remove with a slotted spoon and drain on kitchen paper. Repeat until all the fruit is cooked.

Put the sugar, sesame seeds and 2 tablespoons of the hot oil into a medium saucepan and heat gently until the sugar melts and begins to caramelise. Do not let it get too hot or boil. When it is light brown, add the fruit sections a few at a time to prevent them sticking and stir them gently in the caramel syrup to coat them.

Lift them carefully out on to a plate and allow them to harden for a minute or two before serving.

TIP

Both oil and sugar are volatile when hot, so care should be taken: water must never be added to either until the mixture has cooled.

Lemon Sponge Cake v *UK*

MAKES 2 X 18-CM/7-INCH ROUNDS

CAKE

250g/9oz plain flour
1½ tbsp baking powder
90g/3¼oz unrefined caster sugar
3 lemons, zest and juice
125g/4½oz margarine
75ml/2½fl oz hot water
25ml/1fl oz malt extract

ICING

50g/2oz margarine
115g/4oz unrefined icing sugar
1 tsp grated lemon zest
2 tsp single soya cream

FILLING

4 tbsp apricot jam
walnuts, finely chopped

Preparation time:
25 minutes

Cooking time:
25 minutes

Grease and line 2 x 18-cm/7-inch cake tins.

To make the cake, sift the flour, baking powder and sugar into a large bowl and add the lemon zest. In a small bowl, combine the water, malt extract and lemon juice. Add to the flour mixture, beat for a few minutes until smooth then transfer to the prepared tins. Bake at 200°C/400°F/gas 6 for 25 minutes until just firm and golden brown.

Meanwhile, make the icing by beating together the margarine, sugar, zest and cream. Beat well, until light and fluffy.

Sandwich the two cakes together with apricot jam and half the icing. Spread the remaining icing on top and sprinkle with walnuts.

Pecan Macaroons ~ *USA*

Pecans are absolutely my favourite nuts and I just love them in this recipe as these macaroons melt in the mouth.

MAKES 20

4 large free-range egg whites
350g/12oz unrefined caster sugar
350g/12oz pecans, chopped

115g/4oz fresh white breadcrumbs
1 tsp vanilla essence

Preparation time:
25 minutes

Cooking time:
20–25 minutes

In a large bowl, whisk the egg whites until they are stiff and then whisk in the sugar a little at a time until they become glossy. Divide the mixture between two bowls. Stir the nuts and breadcrumbs into one and the vanilla essence into the other.

Spread the nut and crumb mixture on a floured surface and press it flat until it is about 5-mm/¼-inch thick. Cut out 20 rounds with a pastry cutter. Lay the rounds on a greased baking tray and spread each one with some of the reserved vanilla mixture. Bake at 170°C/325°F/gas 3 for 20–25 minutes or until lightly browned. Leave to cool on the tray.

Lemon Wafers v *Spain*

Preparation time:
15 minutes

Cooking time:
8–10 minutes

Lemon has always been one of my favourite flavours and I use it whenever and wherever I can in my cooking. These light and crisp biscuits are just right for serving with ice-cream or sorbet.

MAKES ABOUT 28

115g/4oz butter or margarine, softened
115g/4oz unrefined caster sugar
115g/4oz plain flour

½ tsp ground ginger
3 tbsp fresh lemon juice

In a medium bowl cream the butter or margarine and sugar until it is light and fluffy. Sift the flour and ginger together, add half to the creamed mixture with the lemon juice and beat again. Then add the remaining flour and beat well.

Place teaspoonsful of the mixture on two well-greased baking trays. Leave plenty of room between them, as they spread to about double their size.

Bake at 190°C/375°F/gas 5 for 8–10 minutes. The edges should be crisp and the middle pale in colour. Remove them from the baking tray and allow them to cool on a wire rack before lifting them off carefully with a knife.

Butter Crunch Squares ~ *UK*

Preparation time:
20–25 minutes

Cooking time:
25–30 minutes

These squares are almost like flapjacks but they have an extra crumbly topping.

MAKES 18

350g/12oz plain flour
225g/8oz butter or margarine
140g/5oz unrefined caster sugar
4 tsp ground cinnamon

2 egg yolks and 1 egg white from medium free-range eggs
225g/8oz pecans, coarsely chopped

Sift the flour into a large bowl. Rub in the butter or margarine and stir in 85g/3oz of the sugar. Stir in 3 teaspoons of the cinnamon and the egg yolks.

Divide the mixture between two buttered shallow 23-cm/9-inch square tins and press down lightly. Brush the surfaces with lightly beaten egg white. Top with the nuts mixed with the remaining sugar and cinnamon. Bake at 180°C/350°F/gas 4 for 20–25 minutes.

Cut into squares while still warm and allow to cool in the pan. Lift out carefully before they are quite cold.

Chocolate Crescents V *Mexico*

These crunchy chocolate biscuits taste good in any shape you like – crescents, diamonds or hearts.

Preparation time:
20–25 minutes

Cooking time:
20 minutes

MAKES APPROXIMATELY 20

140g/5oz plain flour, sifted
50g/2oz unrefined caster sugar
pinch of sea salt
85g/3oz butter or margarine

50g/2oz almonds, toasted (page 70)
 and chopped
50g/2oz plain chocolate, grated
1–2 tbsp soya or dairy milk

In a large bowl sift the flour with the sugar and a pinch of salt. Rub in the butter or margarine and work it with your fingers until it resembles coarse breadcrumbs.

Add the almonds and the chocolate, and continue to work the mixture until it forms a smooth dough adding a little milk if necessary.

Roll out the dough thinly on a lightly floured surface and cut it into your desired shape with a cutter. Re-roll the trimmings as necessary.

Bake the shapes on a greased baking tray at 160°C/325°F/gas 3 for 18–20 minutes. Allow them to cool on a wire rack.

Poppy Seed Cookies V *Germany*

These satisfying biscuits are particularly good when half-dipped in chocolate.

Preparation time:
30 minutes

Cooking time:
20 minutes

MAKES 24

75ml/2½fl oz dairy or soya milk
115g/4oz poppy seeds
50g/2oz butter or margarine
50g/2oz unrefined caster sugar
25g/1oz plain chocolate, melted

½ tsp ground cinnamon
¼ tsp ground cloves
115g/4oz currants
140g/5oz plain flour
1 tsp baking powder

In a small saucepan, heat the milk until almost boiling, then remove the pan from the heat and soak the poppy seeds in the milk for about 15 minutes.

In a medium bowl, cream the butter or margarine with the sugar until it is light and fluffy, then add the melted chocolate, spices, currants and the poppy seed mixture.

Sift in the flour and baking powder and knead to form a pliable dough. Roll the dough into 24 small balls and place on a greased baking sheet, then press them down lightly with a fork.

Bake the cookies at 180°C/350°F/gas 4 for 20 minutes until they turn crisp, then allow them to cool on a wire rack.

Top to bottom:
Butter Crunch Squares,
Chocolate Crescents and
Poppy Seed Cookies

MENU PLANNERS

These menus are intended to help you plan a successful meal. Remember to adjust each individual recipe quantity to suit the number of people you are cooking for.

Greek Menu

(see photograph on pages 108–9)

Melizanasalata (page 24)
served with warmed pitta bread

....

Spanokopitta (page 106)

Potatoes with Lemon (page 129)

Warm Courgette Salad (page 66)

Cephalonian Salad (page 55)

....

Spiced Fruit Filo Parcels (page 156)
served with Greek yoghurt

Italian Menu

Ravioli and Spinach Broth (page 40)

....

Fontina and Tomato Pie (page 96)

Roasted Mushrooms with
Peperonata (page 135)

Fennel and Rocket Salad (page 50)

....

Panna Cotta with Raspberry Coulis
(page 166)

Lemon Wafers (page 181)

Mexican Menu

Black Bean Soup (page 42)

....

Red Enchiladas (page 88) with
Salsa Verde (page 150)

Spicy Sweetcorn (page 137)

A simple green salad with avocado
served with Classic Vinaigrette (page 151)
made with lime juice

....

Sopapillas (page 157)

French Menu

Artichoke, Goats' Cheese and
Walnut Salad (page 57)

....

Quiche Linda (page 113)

Fine Beans with Almonds (page 132)

....

Warm Chocolate Soufflés with
Bittersweet Sauce (page 176)

Spring Menu ∨

Avocado Hummus (page 22)
served with a
selection of fresh vegetable sticks

....

Asparagus and Lemon Risotto (page 114)

Rocket and Alfalfa Salad (page 66)

....

Rhubarb Fool (page 158)

Summer Menu

Chilled Red Pepper and Lime
Soup (page 42)

....

Pesto Genovese with
Green Beans and Potato (page 68)

Surfers' Salad (page 57)

....

Pecan Roulade (page 163)

Autumn Menu ∨

Vegetable Soup with Coconut (page 38)

....

Chickpea and Okra Stir-fry (page 80)

Grilled Spicy Tofu (page 101)

....

Tarte Tatin (page 173)

Winter Menu

Chilli Corn Fritters (page 24) served with
Garlic Dipping Sauce (page 147)

....

Green Curry (page 102)
served with jasmine, basmati or
plain boiled rice

....

Pear Flan (page 175)

Menu Planners

(continued)

Birthday Celebration

Baked Portobello Mushrooms
(page 77)

....

Minted Couscous with
Roasted Vegetables (page 105)

Lettuce Hearts with Avocado, Croûtons
and Blue Cheese Dressing (page 50)

....

Fruit Soufflés (page 165)

Pecan Macaroons (page 180)

Children's Party

A selection of sandwiches (page 82–3)
and pizza slices (page 116–20)

....

Savoury Puff Pastry Rolls (page 19)

Oven Potato Chips (page 128)

Dishes of cherry tomatoes
and a selection of fresh vegetable sticks

....

Ice-cream Cake (page 158)
served with baby bananas
and seedless grapes

Chocolate Crescents (page 182)

Easter Menu

Warm Puy Lentils
on a Bed of Rocket (page 65)

....

Traditional Artichoke Pie (page 107)

Mediterranean-style Green Beans
(page 142)

Lemon Spinach (page 140)

....

Naughty Nougat Cake (page 169)

Midsummer's Eve Picnic

Cucumber, Quark and Dill Soup
(page 33)

....

Caponata (page 23)
served with bread sticks

Felafels (page 29) served with
Yoghurt with Fresh Mint (page 147)
and pitta bread

Broccoli and Parmesan Tartlets (page 22)

Creole Spinach and Hot Pepper
Salad (page 62)

Nutty Wild Rice Salad with
Citrus Dressing (page 60)

....

Fruit Flan (page 156)

Candlelit Dinner

French Onion Soup (page 37)

....

Asparagus Crêpes with Tarragon and
Crème Fraîche (page 20)

Watercress Salad with Mushrooms
and Gruyère (page 54)

....

Non-dairy Crème Brulée (page 178)

Oriental Feast V

(see photograph on pages 72–3)

Spring Rolls (page 30) with
Ginger Dipping Sauce (page 146)
and Sweet and Sour
Chilli Dipping Sauce (page 146)

....

Spicy Tofu (page 71)

Aromatic Vegetable Stir-fry (page 71)

Pad Thai Noodles (page 94)

Special Fried Rice (page 142)

Sweet and Sour Cucumber Salad (page 58)

Crispy Fried Seaweed (page 138)

....

Toffee Apples and Bananas (page 179)

Coconut Rice Pudding (page 160)

Thanksgiving Meal

Tomato and Rosemary Soup (page 45)
served with Croûtons (page 152)

....

Festive Loaf (page 113)

Herby Stuffing (page 153)
served with Special Gravy (page 149)

Oven-roasted Vegetable Chips with
Whole Garlic (page 137)

Glazed Carrots with Honey and
Sesame Seeds (page 137)

Minted Peas (page 138)

....

Grandma's Apple Pie (page 161)

Christmas Meal

Broccoli and Stilton Soup (page 36)

....

Mushroom Roast (page 124) served with
Onion and Juniper Gravy (page 151)
and Cranberry Sauce (page 148)

Chestnut Stuffing (page 153)

Herby Potato Cakes (page 130)

Brussels Sprouts with Chestnuts (page 141)

....

Celebration Pudding (page 172)
served with Crème Anglaise (page 170)

INDEX